MATHEMATICAL DYNAMICS OF ECONOMIC MARKETS

MATHEMATICAL DYNAMICS OF ECONOMIC MARKETS

ALEXEI KROUGLOV

Nova Science Publishers, Inc.
New York

LIBRARY OF CONGRESS CATALOGING-IN-PUBLICATION DATA

Krouglov, Alexei.
Mathematical dynamics of economic markets / Alexei Krouglov.
p. cm.
Includes index.
ISBN 1-59454-528-6
1. Business cycles--Mathematical models. 2. Finance--Mathematical models. 3. Investments--Mathematical models. 4. Arbitrage--Mathematical models. I. Title.
HB3711.K836 2005
330'.01'5195--dc22 2005023396

Published by Nova Science Publishers, Inc. ✣ New York

CONTENTS

Chapter 1

REAL BUSINESS CYCLES

1.1 INTRODUCTION

In this Chapter I am going to describe the mathematical model of real business fluctuations. Model is described by the system of second-order ordinary differential equations. The fluctuations are resulted as a solution of the differential equations.

I am going to present here few models. The first one is a model, which shows the market with one product and one supplier. For this case I describe the basic relationships connecting the product's supply, demand, and prices. I demonstrate dynamics how the economic system, which was forced to leave the equilibrium state, goes to new one. The second model portrays the situation, where market has one product and two suppliers. For this case I describe how the economic system, which contains two competing suppliers, is trying to rebalance itself and find the equilibrium state. The third one is a model, where market has n products and n suppliers. For this case I use the classic Input-Output Model, show dynamics of the economic system approaching the equilibrium state, and discuss the limitations of mentioned model to describe such situation.

Originally the content of this Chapter was described in [4] – [6], [8], [10].

1.2 BASICS OF REAL BUSINESS FLUCTUATIONS

1.2.1 Initial Equilibrium

Let me consider model with one product (for example, commodity). In this section I assume that the product's demand $V_D(t)$ is developing with the fixed rate r_D^0 and describe the dynamics of the product's supply $V_S(t)$.

At the beginning I assume that market had been in equilibrium position until some point in time $t = t_0$, that means that the volumes of product's supply and demand on market were equal, i.e. they both were developing with constant rate r_D^0.

$$V_D(t) = r_D^0 \, t + V_D^0 \tag{1.1}$$

$$V_S(t) = V_D(t) \tag{1.2}$$

Let me assume that at some point in time $t = t_0$ the equilibrium situation is broken because of whatever the circumstances,

$$V_S(t_0) = V_D(t_0) \pm \Delta , \tag{1.3}$$

where $\Delta > 0$.

How in that situation the system would come to the new equilibrium position?

1.2.2 Supply Forces

Actually I am about to make the first assumption for dynamics of economic forces.

Hypothesis 1 Behavior of Product's Supply Force

When the volumes of product's demand and supply are not equal, it creates the disturbing "supply force", which affects the rate of product's supply. The changes in the rate of product's supply at each point in time are inversely-linearly proportional to the product's surplus (or shortage) on the market.

Mathematically the statement above can be described as the following expression.

$$\frac{d^2 V_S(t)}{dt^2} = -\lambda \left(V_S(t) - V_D(t) \right) \tag{1.4}$$

where $\lambda > 0$.

Thus I have obtained the second-order ordinary differential equation regarding to the volume of product's supply $V_S(t)$, which can be resolved (see for example, [19]).

The solution for $V_S(t)$ is so-called equation of *harmonic oscillations* and is shown below for $t > t_0$ (together with formula for $V_D(t)$).

$$V_D(t) = r_D^0 \, t + V_D^0 \tag{1.5}$$

$$V_S(t) = \pm \Delta \cos\left(\sqrt{\lambda}\,(t - t_0)\right) + \frac{r_D^0}{\sqrt{\lambda}} \sin\left(\sqrt{\lambda}\,(t - t_0)\right) + r_D^0 \, t + V_D^0 \tag{1.6}$$

What would happen with dynamics of the volumes of product's supply and demand if I relax the previous assumption that the product's demand is developing with the fixed rate after the system has left the state of equilibrium?

1.2.3 Demand Forces

Here I am about to make the second assumption for dynamics of economic forces.

Hypothesis 2 Behavior of Product's Demand Force

When the volumes of product's demand and supply are not equal, it creates the disturbing "demand force", which affects the rate of product's demand. The changes in the rate of product's demand at each point in time are linearly proportional to the changes in product's surplus (or shortage) on the market.

Mathematically the statement above means the following.

$$\frac{d^2V_D(t)}{dt^2} = \mu\frac{d}{dt}\left(V_S(t) - V_D(t)\right) \tag{1.7}$$

where $\mu > 0$.

Let me now combine the Hypotheses 1 and 2 together. If I subtract the Equation (1.7) from Equation (1.4) I will obtain the following second-order ordinary differential equation regarding to the volume of product's surplus (or shortage) $\left[V_S(t) - V_D(t)\right]$.

$$\frac{d^2}{dt^2}\left(V_S(t) - V_D(t)\right) + \mu\frac{d}{dt}\left(V_S(t) - V_D(t)\right) + \lambda\left(V_S(t) - V_D(t)\right) = 0 \tag{1.8}$$

This is so-called equation of *free oscillations*, which can be resolved (see for example, [19]).

At first, the roots of characteristic equation corresponding to Equation (1.8) are,

$$k_{1,2} = -\frac{\mu}{2} \pm \sqrt{\frac{\mu^2}{4} - \lambda} \tag{1.9}$$

And the solution for $\left[V_S(t) - V_D(t)\right]$ is shown below for $t > t_0$.

(a) If $\frac{\mu^2}{4} > \lambda$ the solution of Equation (1.8) is,

$$V_S(t) - V_D(t) = C_1 \exp\{k_1(t - t_0)\} + C_2 \exp\{k_2(t - t_0)\}, \tag{1.10}$$

where $C_1 = \pm\frac{\Delta}{2}\left(\frac{\mu}{2\sqrt{\frac{\mu^2}{4} - \lambda}} + 1\right)$ and $C_2 = \pm\frac{\Delta}{2}\left(\frac{-\mu}{2\sqrt{\frac{\mu^2}{4} - \lambda}} + 1\right)$.

(b) If $\frac{\mu^2}{4} = \lambda$ the solution of Equation (1.8) is,

$$V_S(t) - V_D(t) = (C_1 + C_2(t - t_0))\exp\left\{-\frac{\mu}{2}(t - t_0)\right\}, \quad (1.11)$$

where $C_1 = \pm\Delta$ and $C_2 = \dfrac{\pm\Delta\mu}{2}$.

(c) If $\dfrac{\mu^2}{4} < \lambda$ the solution of Equation (1.8) is,

$$V_S(t) - V_D(t) = \exp\left\{-\frac{\mu}{2}(t - t_0)\right\} \times \left(C_1 \cos\left(\sqrt{\lambda - \frac{\mu^2}{4}}(t - t_0)\right) + C_2 \sin\left(\sqrt{\lambda - \frac{\mu^2}{4}}(t - t_0)\right)\right), \quad (1.12)$$

where $C_1 = \pm\Delta$ and $C_2 = \dfrac{\pm\Delta\mu}{2\sqrt{\lambda - \frac{\mu^2}{4}}}$.

The solution represented here by Equation (1.12) is the so-called *damped oscillations*. Similar calculations can be carried out if the equilibrium situation is broken because of,

$$r_S(t_0) = r_D(t_0) \pm \delta, \quad (1.13)$$

1.3 Condition of Non-Negativity

For conciliation of the model with reality I have to impose the non-negativity conditions on the volumes of the product's demand and supply, i.e. $V_D(t) \geq 0$ and $V_S(t) \geq 0$.

The non-negativity conditions bring small changes in the results described in the previous section.

I will illustrate these changes with the same example that I used earlier.

As before, I consider model with one product, assume that the product's demand $V_D(t)$ is developing with the fixed rate r_D^0 and describe the dynamics of the product's supply $V_S(t)$.

The market had been in equilibrium position until time $t = t_0$, the volumes of product's supply and demand on market were equal, and they both were developing with constant rate r_D^0.

$$V_D(t) = r_D^0 t + V_D^0 \quad (1.14)$$

$$V_S(t) = V_D(t) \quad (1.15)$$

At some point in time $t = t_0$ the equilibrium situation was broken,

$$V_S(t_0) = V_D(t_0) + \Delta, \qquad (1.16)$$

where $\Delta > 0$ and $V_D(t_0) < \Delta$.

I will assume further for simplicity that $r_D^0 \equiv 0$.

As before, I can write the second-order ordinary differential equation regarding to the volume of product's supply $V_S(t)$ and auxiliary condition for it,

$$\frac{d^2V_S(t)}{dt^2} = -\lambda\left(V_S(t) - V_D(t)\right) \qquad (1.17)$$

$$V_S(t) \geq 0 \qquad (1.18)$$

where $\lambda > 0$.

The resulting formulae for $V_D(t)$ and $V_S(t)$ for $t > t_0$ are shown below.

$$V_D(t) = V_D^0 \qquad (1.19)$$

(a) If $t_0 < t \leq t_0 + \frac{1}{\sqrt{\lambda}}\left(\frac{\pi}{2} + \sin^{-1}\frac{V_D^0}{\Delta}\right)$ the solution for $V_S(t)$ is,

$$V_S(t) = \Delta\cos\left(\sqrt{\lambda}\,(t - t_0)\right) + V_D^0 \qquad (1.20)$$

(b) If $t > t_0 + \frac{1}{\sqrt{\lambda}}\left(\frac{\pi}{2} + \sin^{-1}\frac{V_D^0}{\Delta}\right)$ the solution for $V_S(t)$ is,

$$V_S(t) = V_D^0\left(1 - \cos\left(\sqrt{\lambda}\,(t - t_0)\right)\right) \qquad (1.21)$$

The formulae above for $V_S(t)$ tell that for the listed here example the volume of product's supply is harmonically decreasing until it reaches zero, and harmonically fluctuating after that point in time.

1.4 PRICE FLUCTUATIONS

1.4.1 Price as Dual Variable

Let me again consider model with one product and introduce into the model the concept of prices.

At first I want to formally describe the state of equilibrium in the model.

Hypothesis 3 Dynamics in the State of Equilibrium

When there is no disturbing influence in the model, both the product's demand and supply are developing with the fixed rate, and the product's price remains constant.

If somehow the equilibrium state is broken, the system experiences the recovering forces, which are trying to bring it to new equilibrium state. The important role in that process is played by the product's price, which performs the function of dual variable.

Here I make the assumption about dynamics of product's prices $P_R(t)$.

Hypothesis 4 Behavior of Product's Price

When the volumes of product's demand and supply are not equal, it creates the unsettling effect, which changes the product's price. The changes in the product's price at each point in time are inversely-linearly proportional to the product's surplus (or shortage) on the market.

Mathematically the statement above means the following,

$$\frac{dP_R(t)}{dt} = -\lambda_P \left(V_S(t) - V_D(t)\right) \tag{1.22}$$

where $\lambda_P > 0$.

Then Hypotheses 1 and 4 together give the following claim.

Proposition 1 Behavior of Product's Supply with Respect to Price

The changes in the rate of product's supply at each point in time are linearly proportional to the changes in the product's price on the market.

Mathematically it means the following,

$$\frac{d^2V_S(t)}{dt^2} = \lambda_S \frac{dP_R(t)}{dt} \tag{1.23}$$

where $\lambda_S > 0$.

Similarly Hypotheses 2 and 4 produce the following claim.

Proposition 2 Behavior of Product's Demand with Respect to Price

The changes in the rate of product's demand at each point in time are inversely-linearly proportional to the changes in the rate of the product's price on the market.

Mathematically it means the following,

$$\frac{d^2V_D(t)}{dt^2} = -\lambda_D \frac{d^2P_R(t)}{dt^2} \tag{1.24}$$

where $\lambda_D > 0$.

Using just introduced notation I can replace preceding Equation (1.8) – second-order ordinary differential equation about the volume of product's surplus (or shortage) $\left[V_S(t) - V_D(t)\right]$ with the following one.

$$\frac{d^2}{dt^2}(V_S(t)-V_D(t))+\lambda_P\,\lambda_D\,\frac{d}{dt}(V_S(t)-V_D(t))+\lambda_P\,\lambda_S\,(V_S(t)-V_D(t))=0 \tag{1.25}$$

1.4.2 Duality of Price Fluctuations

Thus for economic model with one product, we have the following system of ordinary differential equations connecting at each point in time the product's demand $V_D(t)$, the product's supply $V_S(t)$, and the product's price $P_R(t)$,

$$\frac{dP_R(t)}{dt}=-\lambda_P\,(V_S(t)-V_D(t)) \tag{1.26}$$

$$\frac{d^2V_S(t)}{dt^2}=\lambda_S\,\frac{dP_R(t)}{dt} \tag{1.27}$$

$$\frac{d^2V_D(t)}{dt^2}=-\lambda_D\,\frac{d^2P_R(t)}{dt^2} \tag{1.28}$$

Let me differentiate Equation (1.28) and integrate both Equation (1.27) and Equation (1.28). Therefore I obtain the following result,

$$\frac{d^2P_R(t)}{dt^2}=-\lambda_P\,\frac{d}{dt}(V_S(t)-V_D(t)) \tag{1.29}$$

$$\frac{dV_S(t)}{dt}=\lambda_S\,P_R(t)+C_1 \tag{1.30}$$

$$\frac{dV_D(t)}{dt}=-\lambda_D\,\frac{dP_R(t)}{dt}+C_2 \tag{1.31}$$

where C_1 and C_2 are integration's constants.

I subtract Equation (1.31) from Equation (1.30), and use the resulted difference in Equation (1.29). Thus I obtain the following second-order ordinary differential equation expressing the behavior of the product's price $P_R(t)$,

$$\frac{d^2P_R(t)}{dt^2}+\lambda_P\,\lambda_D\,\frac{dP_R(t)}{dt}+\lambda_P\,\lambda_S\,P_R(t)+C_3=0 \tag{1.32}$$

where $C_3=\lambda_P\,(C_1-C_2)$ is a constant.

The constant C_3 serves for reconciliation between ordinary variables $V_S(t)$ and $V_D(t)$, and dual variable $P_R(t)$ at initial time $t = t_0$.

As an example I consider again model with one product, assume that the market had been in equilibrium position until time $t = t_0$, the volumes of product's supply $V_S(t)$ and demand $V_D(t)$ on market were equal, and they both were developing with constant rate r_D^0.

$$V_D(t) = r_D^0 (t - t_0) + V_D^0 \tag{1.33}$$

$$V_S(t) = V_D(t) \tag{1.34}$$

where $V_D(t_0) = V_D^0$.

At some point in time $t = t_0$ the equilibrium situation was broken,

$$V_S(t_0) = V_D(t_0) \pm \Delta\,, \tag{1.35}$$

As earlier I assume for simplicity that the product's demand $V_D(t)$ continues to develop with the fixed rate r_D^0 for $t > t_0$. That assumption implies that it holds $\lambda_D = 0$. Then I describe the dynamics of the product's prices $P_R(t)$ based on Equation (1.32).

Since $\lambda_D = 0$ Equation (1.32) transforms into the following,

$$\frac{d^2 P_R(t)}{dt^2} + \lambda_P\, \lambda_S\, P_R(t) + C_3 = 0 \tag{1.36}$$

or using new variable $P_1(t) = P_R(t) + \dfrac{C_3}{\lambda_P\, \lambda_S}$,

$$\frac{d^2 P_1(t)}{dt^2} + \lambda_P\, \lambda_S\, P_1(t) = 0 \tag{1.37}$$

The initial conditions for $P_R(t)$ are $P_R(t_0) = P_R^0$ and $\dfrac{dP_R(t_0)}{dt} = \mp \Delta\, \lambda_P$ from Equation (1.26). Therefore the initial conditions for $P_1(t)$ are $P_1(t_0) = P_R^0 + \dfrac{C_3}{\lambda_P\, \lambda_S}$ and $\dfrac{dP_1(t_0)}{dt} = \mp \Delta\, \lambda_P$.

Thus the solution for $P_1(t)$ (and respectively for $P_R(t)$) for $t \geq t_0$ is the equation of *harmonic oscillations* (see [19]). Solution for $P_R(t)$ is shown below,

$$P_R(t)=\left(P_R^0+\frac{C_3}{\lambda_P\,\lambda_S}\right)\cos\left(\sqrt{\lambda_P\,\lambda_S}\,(t-t_0)\right)\mp\Delta\sqrt{\frac{\lambda_P}{\lambda_S}}\sin\left(\sqrt{\lambda_P\,\lambda_S}\,(t-t_0)\right)-\frac{C_3}{\lambda_P\,\lambda_S} \quad (1.38)$$

Since $C_3=\lambda_P\left(C_1-C_2\right)$, $C_1=r_D^0-\lambda_S\,P_R^0$, $C_2=r_D^0\mp\Delta\,\lambda_P\,\lambda_D$ and $\lambda_D=0$, it holds

$$C_3=-\lambda_P\,\lambda_S\,P_R^0, \quad (1.39)$$

and I rewrite Equation (1.38) into the following form

$$P_R(t)=P_R^0\mp\Delta\sqrt{\frac{\lambda_P}{\lambda_S}}\sin\left(\sqrt{\lambda_P\,\lambda_S}\,(t-t_0)\right) \quad (1.40)$$

Let me conclude this part with finding of initial price $P_R(t_0)=P_R^0$ for this example that guarantees that the product's price always resides in the positive domain.

It is seen that $P_R(t)\ge 0$ for $t>t_0$ when

$$\left(P_R(t)\right)_{\min}=P_R^0-\Delta\sqrt{\frac{\lambda_P}{\lambda_S}}\ge 0, \quad (1.41)$$

and hence for

$$P_R^0\ge\left(P_R^0\right)_{\min}=\Delta\sqrt{\frac{\lambda_P}{\lambda_S}} \quad (1.42)$$

required inequality $P_R(t)\ge 0$ takes place for $t>t_0$.

Otherwise it is required to hold the non-negativity condition for dual variable $P_R(t)$ similar to previously discussed non-negativity requirements for ordinary variables $V_S(t)$ and $V_D(t)$.

1.5 Intra-Industrial Dynamics

1.5.1 Model Assumptions

To describe the appearance of intra-industrial fluctuations I will consider an economical model with one product, which is produced by two business entities.

But before to proceed I make an assumption about dynamics of multiple supply forces.

Hypothesis 5 Behavior of Multiple Supply Forces

When there are multiple "supply forces" acting on the market, their impacts are summed.

Mathematically it means the following,

$$\frac{d^2V_S(t)}{dt^2} = \frac{d^2V_{S1}(t)}{dt^2} + \frac{d^2V_{S2}(t)}{dt^2} + \cdots = \sum_{i=1}^{\infty} \frac{d^2V_{Si}(t)}{dt^2}$$

As earlier I assume that the market had been in equilibrium position until time $t = t_0$, the volumes of product's supply $V_S(t)$ and demand $V_D(t)$ on market were equal, and they both were developing with constant rate r_D^0.

$$V_D(t) = r_D^0 t + V_D^0 \tag{1.43}$$

$$V_S(t) = V_D(t) \tag{1.44}$$

Additional requirement here is that the total product's supply is provided and the total product's demand is satisfied by two independent business entities,

$$V_S(t) = V_{S1}(t) + V_{S2}(t) \tag{1.45}$$

$$r_D^0 = r_{S1}^0 + r_{S2}^0 \tag{1.46}$$

I will describe below the effects of few different scenarios.

1.5.2 Effect of Exit from Market

At this situation I assume that at some point in time $t = t_0$ the equilibrium situation was broken, because one of two business entities has decided to exit the market and stopped the commodity's supply,

$$r_{S2}(t) = \begin{cases} r_{S2}^0, & t < t_0 \\ 0, & t \geq t_0 \end{cases} \tag{1.47}$$

That event creates the product's shortage on the market, which starts building with the following rate $[r_S(t) - r_D(t)]$,

$$r_S(t) - r_D(t) = r_{S1}(t) - r_D(t) \tag{1.48}$$

where $t > t_0$ and $r_S(t_0) - r_D(t_0) = -r_{S2}^0$.

Now I produce the system of ordinary differential equations connecting at each point in time the product's demand $V_D(t)$, the product's supply $V_{S1}(t)$, and the product's price $P_R(t)$,

$$\frac{dP_R(t)}{dt} = -\lambda_P \left(V_{S1}(t) - V_D(t)\right) \tag{1.49}$$

$$\frac{d^2 V_{S1}(t)}{dt^2} = \lambda_{S1} \frac{dP_R(t)}{dt} \tag{1.50}$$

$$\frac{d^2 V_D(t)}{dt^2} = -\lambda_D \frac{d^2 P_R(t)}{dt^2} \tag{1.51}$$

where $t > t_0$.

I replace preceding Equations (1.49 – 51) with the following second-order ordinary differential equation about the volume of product's surplus (or shortage) $\left[V_{S1}(t) - V_D(t)\right]$,

$$\frac{d^2}{dt^2}\left(V_{S1}(t) - V_D(t)\right) + \lambda_P \lambda_D \frac{d}{dt}\left(V_{S1}(t) - V_D(t)\right) + \lambda_P \lambda_{S1}\left(V_{S1}(t) - V_D(t)\right) = 0 \tag{1.52}$$

where $V_{S1}(t_0) - V_D(t_0) = 0$ and $\frac{d}{dt}\left(V_{S1}(t_0) - V_D(t_0)\right) = -r_{S2}^0$.

The roots of characteristic equation corresponding to Equation (1.52) are,

$$k_{1,2} = -\frac{\lambda_P \lambda_D}{2} \pm \sqrt{\frac{\lambda_P^2 \lambda_D^2}{4} - \lambda_P \lambda_{S1}} \tag{1.53}$$

And now I investigate the behavior of $\left[V_{S1}(t) - V_D(t)\right]$ for $t > t_0$ (see [19]).

(a) If $\frac{\lambda_P^2 \lambda_D^2}{4} > \lambda_P \lambda_{S1}$ the solution of Equation (1.52) is,

$$V_{S1}(t) - V_D(t) = C_1 \exp\{k_1 (t - t_0)\} + C_2 \exp\{k_2 (t - t_0)\}, \tag{1.54}$$

where C_1 and C_2 are constants.

Since both $k_1 < 0$ and $k_2 < 0$ it takes place $V_{S1}(t) - V_D(t) \to 0$ for $t \to +\infty$. It means that residual business entity fulfills the product's shortage created by departure of another business entity from the market. Market again comes to the equilibrium state, and the product's supply and demand turns into being equal.

(b) If $\frac{\lambda_P^2 \lambda_D^2}{4} = \lambda_P \lambda_{S1}$ the solution of Equation (1.52) is,

$$V_{S1}(t) - V_D(t) = (C_1 + C_2(t - t_0))\exp\left\{-\frac{\lambda_P \lambda_D}{2}(t - t_0)\right\}, \tag{1.55}$$

where C_1 and C_2 are constants.

Since $\lambda_P \lambda_D > 0$ it takes place $V_{S1}(t) - V_D(t) \to 0$ for $t \to +\infty$. Again the residual business entity fulfills the product's shortage created by departure of another business entity from the market, and market comes to the equilibrium state.

(c) If $\frac{\lambda_P^2 \lambda_D^2}{4} < \lambda_P \lambda_{S1}$ the solution of Equation (1.52) is,

$$\begin{aligned} V_{S1}(t) - V_D(t) &= \exp\left\{-\frac{\lambda_P \lambda_D}{2}(t - t_0)\right\} \\ &\times \left(C_1 \cos\left(\sqrt{\lambda_P \lambda_{S1} - \frac{\lambda_P^2 \lambda_D^2}{4}}\,(t - t_0)\right) + C_2 \sin\left(\sqrt{\lambda_P \lambda_{S1} - \frac{\lambda_P^2 \lambda_D^2}{4}}\,(t - t_0)\right)\right) \end{aligned} \tag{1.56}$$

where C_1 and C_2 are constants.

Since $\lambda_P \lambda_D > 0$ it takes place $V_{S1}(t) - V_D(t) \to 0$ for $t \to +\infty$. Again the residual business entity fulfills the product's shortage created by departure of another business entity from the market, and market comes to the equilibrium state.

1.5.3 Effect of Demand Growth

Here I assume that the product's demand is increasing at some point in time $t = t_0$ with a constant rate $\delta > 0$,

$$r_D(t) = \begin{cases} r_D^0, & t < t_0 \\ r_D^0 + \delta, & t = t_0 \end{cases} \tag{1.57}$$

That event creates the product's shortage on the market, which starts building with the following rate $[r_S(t)-r_D(t)]$, where $t>t_0$ and $r_S(t_0)-r_D(t_0)=-\delta$.

Here is the system of ordinary differential equations connecting at each point in time the product's demand $V_D(t)$, the product's supply $V_{S1}(t)+V_{S2}(t)$, and the product's price $P_R(t)$,

$$\frac{dP_R(t)}{dt}=-\lambda_P(V_S(t)-V_D(t)) \tag{1.58}$$

$$V_S(t)=V_{S1}(t)+V_{S2}(t) \tag{1.59}$$

$$\frac{d^2V_{S1}(t)}{dt^2}=\lambda_{S1}\frac{dP_R(t)}{dt} \tag{1.60}$$

$$\frac{d^2V_{S2}(t)}{dt^2}=\lambda_{S2}\frac{dP_R(t)}{dt} \tag{1.61}$$

$$\frac{d^2V_D(t)}{dt^2}=-\lambda_D\frac{d^2P_R(t)}{dt^2} \tag{1.62}$$

where $t>t_0$.

The preceding Equations (1.58 – 62) can be replaced with the following second-order ordinary differential equation about the volume of product's surplus (or shortage) $[V_S(t)-V_D(t)]$,

$$\frac{d^2}{dt^2}(V_S(t)-V_D(t))+\lambda_P\lambda_D\frac{d}{dt}(V_S(t)-V_D(t))+\lambda_P(\lambda_{S1}+\lambda_{S2})(V_S(t)-V_D(t))=0 \tag{1.63}$$

where $V_S(t_0)-V_D(t_0)=0$ and $\frac{d}{dt}(V_S(t_0)-V_D(t_0))=-\delta$.

The roots of characteristic equation corresponding to Equation (1.63) are,

$$k_{1,2}=-\frac{\lambda_P\lambda_D}{2}\pm\sqrt{\frac{\lambda_P^2\lambda_D^2}{4}-\lambda_P(\lambda_{S1}+\lambda_{S2})} \tag{1.64}$$

The examination of these roots shows (in the same way as before) that it takes place relationship $V_S(t)-V_D(t)\to 0$ for $t\to+\infty$. It means that business entities collectively fulfill the product's shortage created by the growth in the product's demand on the market.

Market again comes to the equilibrium state, and the product's supply and demand becomes equal.

To calculate the contributions into elimination of the product's shortage from each individual business entity I will solve Equation (1.63) and use the following formulae,

$$\frac{d^2V_{S1}(t)}{dt^2} = -\lambda_P \lambda_{S1} \left(V_S(t) - V_D(t)\right) \tag{1.65}$$

$$\frac{d^2V_{S2}(t)}{dt^2} = -\lambda_P \lambda_{S2} \left(V_S(t) - V_D(t)\right) \tag{1.66}$$

(a) If $\frac{\lambda_P^2 \lambda_D^2}{4} > \lambda_P \left(\lambda_{S1} + \lambda_{S2}\right)$ the solution of Equation (1.63) is,

$$V_S(t) - V_D(t) = C_1 \exp\{k_1 (t - t_0)\} + C_2 \exp\{k_2 (t - t_0)\}, \tag{1.67}$$

where $C_1 = -\frac{\delta}{2\sqrt{\frac{\lambda_P^2 \lambda_D^2}{4} - \lambda_P \left(\lambda_{S1} + \lambda_{S2}\right)}}$ and $C_2 = \frac{\delta}{2\sqrt{\frac{\lambda_P^2 \lambda_D^2}{4} - \lambda_P \left(\lambda_{S1} + \lambda_{S2}\right)}}$.

Since $V_{S1}(t_0) = V_{S1}^0$ and $\frac{dV_{S1}(t_0)}{dt} = r_{S1}^0$ it takes place from Equation (1.65),

$$\frac{d^2V_{S1}(t)}{dt^2} = -\lambda_P \lambda_{S1} C_1 \exp\{k_1 (t - t_0)\} - \lambda_P \lambda_{S1} C_2 \exp\{k_2 (t - t_0)\}, \tag{1.68}$$

$$\frac{dV_{S1}(t)}{dt} = -\lambda_P \lambda_{S1} \frac{C_1}{k_1} \exp\{k_1 (t - t_0)\} - \lambda_P \lambda_{S1} \frac{C_2}{k_2} \exp\{k_2 (t - t_0)\} + C_3, \tag{1.69}$$

$$V_{S1}(t) = -\lambda_P \lambda_{S1} \frac{C_1}{k_1^2} \exp\{k_1 (t - t_0)\} - \lambda_P \lambda_{S1} \frac{C_2}{k_2^2} \exp\{k_2 (t - t_0)\} + C_3 (t - t_0) + C_4, \tag{1.70}$$

where $C_3 = r_{S1}^0 + \frac{\lambda_{S1}}{\lambda_{S1} + \lambda_{S2}} \delta$ and $C_4 = V_{S1}^0 - \frac{\lambda_{S1} \lambda_D}{\left(\lambda_{S1} + \lambda_{S2}\right)^2} \delta$.

Thus it takes place for $t \to +\infty$,

$$\frac{dV_{S1}(t)}{dt} \to r_{S1}^0 + \frac{\lambda_{S1}}{\lambda_{S1} + \lambda_{S2}} \delta, \tag{1.71}$$

$$\frac{dV_{S2}(t)}{dt} \to r_{S2}^0 + \frac{\lambda_{S2}}{\lambda_{S1} + \lambda_{S2}}\delta \quad , \tag{1.72}$$

$$\frac{d}{dt}\left(V_{S1}(t) + V_{S2}(t)\right) \to \frac{dV_D(t_0)}{dt} = r_D^0 + \delta \quad , \tag{1.73}$$

(b) If $\frac{\lambda_P^2 \lambda_D^2}{4} = \lambda_P\left(\lambda_{S1} + \lambda_{S2}\right)$ the solution of Equation (1.63) is,

$$V_S(t) - V_D(t) = \left(C_1 + C_2(t - t_0)\right)\exp\left\{-\frac{\lambda_P \lambda_D}{2}(t - t_0)\right\} \quad , \tag{1.74}$$

where $C_1 = 0$ and $C_2 = -\delta$.

Since $V_{S1}(t_0) = V_{S1}^0$ and $\frac{dV_{S1}(t_0)}{dt} = r_{S1}^0$ it takes place from Equation (1.65),

$$\frac{d^2V_{S1}(t)}{dt^2} = \lambda_P \lambda_{S1}\delta(t - t_0)\exp\left\{-\frac{\lambda_P \lambda_D}{2}(t - t_0)\right\} \quad , \tag{1.75}$$

$$\frac{dV_{S1}(t)}{dt} = -\frac{2\lambda_{S1}}{\lambda_D}\delta\left[(t - t_0) + \frac{2}{\lambda_P \lambda_D}\right]\exp\left\{-\frac{\lambda_P \lambda_D}{2}(t - t_0)\right\} + C_3 \quad , \tag{1.76}$$

$$V_{S1}(t) = \frac{\lambda_{S1}}{\lambda_{S1} + \lambda_{S2}}\delta\left[(t - t_0) + \frac{4}{\lambda_P \lambda_D}\right]\exp\left\{-\frac{\lambda_P \lambda_D}{2}(t - t_0)\right\} + C_3(t - t_0) + C_4 \quad , \tag{1.77}$$

where $C_3 = r_{S1}^0 + \frac{\lambda_{S1}}{\lambda_{S1} + \lambda_{S2}}\delta$ and $C_4 = V_{S1}^0 - \frac{\lambda_{S1}\lambda_D}{\left(\lambda_{S1} + \lambda_{S2}\right)^2}\delta$.

Thus it takes place for $t \to +\infty$,

$$\frac{dV_{S1}(t)}{dt} \to r_{S1}^0 + \frac{\lambda_{S1}}{\lambda_{S1} + \lambda_{S2}}\delta \quad , \tag{1.78}$$

$$\frac{dV_{S2}(t)}{dt} \to r_{S2}^0 + \frac{\lambda_{S2}}{\lambda_{S1} + \lambda_{S2}}\delta \quad , \tag{1.79}$$

$$\frac{d}{dt}\left(V_{S1}(t) + V_{S2}(t)\right) \to \frac{dV_D(t_0)}{dt} = r_D^0 + \delta \quad , \tag{1.80}$$

(c) If $\frac{\lambda_P^2 \lambda_D^2}{4} < \lambda_P(\lambda_{S1} + \lambda_{S2})$ the solution of Equation (1.63) is,

$$V_S(t) - V_D(t) = A\exp\left\{-\frac{\lambda_P \lambda_D}{2}(t - t_0)\right\}\sin\left(\sqrt{\lambda_P(\lambda_{S1} + \lambda_{S2}) - \frac{\lambda_P^2 \lambda_D^2}{4}}(t - t_0) + \varphi_0\right) \text{,(1.81}$$

where $A = -\frac{\delta}{\sqrt{\lambda_P(\lambda_{S1} + \lambda_{S2}) - \frac{\lambda_P^2 \lambda_D^2}{4}}}$ and $\varphi_0 = 0$.

Since $V_{S1}(t_0) = V_{S1}^0$ and $\frac{dV_{S1}(t_0)}{dt} = r_{S1}^0$ it takes place from Equation (1.65),

$$\frac{d^2 V_{S1}(t)}{dt^2} = \frac{\lambda_P \lambda_{S1}}{\sqrt{\lambda_P(\lambda_{S1} + \lambda_{S2}) - \frac{\lambda_P^2 \lambda_D^2}{4}}}\delta\exp\left\{-\frac{\lambda_P \lambda_D}{2}(t - t_0)\right\}$$

$$\times\sin\left\{\sqrt{\lambda_P(\lambda_{S1} + \lambda_{S2}) - \frac{\lambda_P^2 \lambda_D^2}{4}}(t - t_0)\right\} \tag{1.82}$$

$$\frac{dV_{S1}(t)}{dt} = \frac{-\lambda_{S1}}{(\lambda_{S1} + \lambda_{S2})\sqrt{\lambda_P(\lambda_{S1} + \lambda_{S2}) - \frac{\lambda_P^2 \lambda_D^2}{4}}}\delta\exp\left\{-\frac{\lambda_P \lambda_D}{2}(t - t_0)\right\}$$

$$\times\left[\begin{array}{l}\sqrt{\lambda_P(\lambda_{S1} + \lambda_{S2}) - \frac{\lambda_P^2 \lambda_D^2}{4}}\cos\left(\sqrt{\lambda_P(\lambda_{S1} + \lambda_{S2}) - \frac{\lambda_P^2 \lambda_D^2}{4}}(t - t_0)\right) \\ + \frac{\lambda_P \lambda_D}{2}\sin\left(\sqrt{\lambda_P(\lambda_{S1} + \lambda_{S2}) - \frac{\lambda_P^2 \lambda_D^2}{4}}(t - t_0)\right)\end{array}\right] + C_3 \tag{1.83}$$

$$V_{S1}(t) = \frac{\lambda_{S1}}{(\lambda_{S1} + \lambda_{S2})^2\sqrt{\lambda_P(\lambda_{S1} + \lambda_{S2}) - \frac{\lambda_P^2 \lambda_D^2}{4}}}\delta\exp\left\{-\frac{\lambda_P \lambda_D}{2}(t - t_0)\right\}$$

$$\times\left[\begin{array}{l}\lambda_D\sqrt{\lambda_P(\lambda_{S1} + \lambda_{S2}) - \frac{\lambda_P^2 \lambda_D^2}{4}}\cos\left(\sqrt{\lambda_P(\lambda_{S1} + \lambda_{S2}) - \frac{\lambda_P^2 \lambda_D^2}{4}}(t - t_0)\right) \\ + \left(\frac{\lambda_P \lambda_D^2}{2} - (\lambda_{S1} + \lambda_{S2})\right)\sin\left(\sqrt{\lambda_P(\lambda_{S1} + \lambda_{S2}) - \frac{\lambda_P^2 \lambda_D^2}{4}}(t - t_0)\right)\end{array}\right] + C_3(t - t_0) + C_4 \tag{1.84}$$

where $C_3 = r_{S1}^0 + \dfrac{\lambda_{S1}}{\lambda_{S1} + \lambda_{S2}}\delta$ and $C_4 = V_{S1}^0 - \dfrac{\lambda_{S1}\lambda_D}{(\lambda_{S1} + \lambda_{S2})^2}\delta$.

Thus it takes place for $t \to +\infty$,

$$\frac{dV_{S1}(t)}{dt} \to r_{S1}^0 + \frac{\lambda_{S1}}{\lambda_{S1} + \lambda_{S2}}\delta, \tag{1.85}$$

$$\frac{dV_{S2}(t)}{dt} \to r_{S2}^0 + \frac{\lambda_{S2}}{\lambda_{S1} + \lambda_{S2}}\delta, \tag{1.86}$$

$$\frac{d}{dt}\left(V_{S1}(t) + V_{S2}(t)\right) \to \frac{dV_D(t_0)}{dt} = r_D^0 + \delta, \tag{1.87}$$

1.5.4 Effect of Attempt to Takeover

In this scenario I assume that a stronger business entity supplies the excessive amount of product on the market for some period of time. It drives the product's price down, and the second business entity starts to decrease its share of the product's supply. Eventually the first business entity finishes supplying excessive amount of product, and market comes to equilibrium state. As a result a stronger business entity increases its share on market for the product.

Formally,

$$r_{S1}(t) = \begin{cases} r_{S1}^0, & t < t_0 \\ r_{S1}^0 + \delta, & t_0 \le t < t_1 \end{cases} \tag{1.88}$$

where $\delta > 0$.

That event creates the product's surplus on the market, which starts building with the following rate $[r_S(t) - r_D(t)]$, where $t > t_0$ and $r_S(t_0) - r_D(t_0) = \delta$.

Here is the system of ordinary differential equations connecting at each point in time the product's demand $V_D(t)$, the product's supply $V_{S1}(t) + V_{S2}(t)$, and the product's price $P_R(t)$,

$$\frac{dP_R(t)}{dt} = -\lambda_P\left(V_S(t) - V_D(t)\right) \tag{1.89}$$

$$V_S(t) = V_{S1}(t) + V_{S2}(t) \tag{1.90}$$

$$\frac{dV_{S1}(t)}{dt} = r_{S1}^0 + \delta \tag{1.91}$$

$$\frac{d^2V_{S2}(t)}{dt^2} = \lambda_{S2} \frac{dP_R(t)}{dt} \tag{1.92}$$

$$\frac{d^2V_D(t)}{dt^2} = -\lambda_D \frac{d^2P_R(t)}{dt^2} \tag{1.93}$$

where $t_0 \le t < t_1$.

Again I can use the following second-order ordinary differential equation for the volume of product's surplus (or shortage) $[V_S(t) - V_D(t)]$ for $t_0 \le t < t_1$,

$$\frac{d^2}{dt^2}(V_S(t) - V_D(t)) + \lambda_P \lambda_D \frac{d}{dt}(V_S(t) - V_D(t)) + \lambda_P \lambda_{S2} (V_S(t) - V_D(t)) = 0 \tag{1.94}$$

where $V_S(t_0) - V_D(t_0) = 0$ and $\frac{d}{dt}(V_S(t_0) - V_D(t_0)) = \delta$.

When a stronger business entity stops supplying excessive amount of product, the system of ordinary differential equations connecting at each point in time the product's demand $V_D(t)$, the product's supply $V_{S1}(t) + V_{S2}(t)$, and the product's price $P_R(t)$ takes the form,

$$\frac{dP_R(t)}{dt} = -\lambda_P (V_S(t) - V_D(t)) \tag{1.95}$$

$$V_S(t) = V_{S1}(t) + V_{S2}(t) \tag{1.96}$$

$$\frac{d^2V_{S1}(t)}{dt^2} = \lambda_{S1} \frac{dP_R(t)}{dt} \tag{1.97}$$

$$\frac{d^2V_{S2}(t)}{dt^2} = \lambda_{S2} \frac{dP_R(t)}{dt} \tag{1.98}$$

$$\frac{d^2V_D(t)}{dt^2} = -\lambda_D \frac{d^2P_R(t)}{dt^2} \tag{1.99}$$

where $t \ge t_1$.

And the similar equation for the volume of product's surplus (or shortage) $[V_S(t)-V_D(t)]$ for $t \geq t_1$,

$$\frac{d^2}{dt^2}(V_S(t)-V_D(t))+\lambda_P\lambda_D\frac{d}{dt}(V_S(t)-V_D(t))+\lambda_P(\lambda_{S1}+\lambda_{S2})(V_S(t)-V_D(t))=0 \tag{1.100}$$

To find initial conditions for $[V_S(t)-V_D(t)]$ and $\frac{d}{dt}(V_S(t)-V_D(t))$ for Equation (1.100) at time $t=t_1$ I have to find the final values for $[V_S(t)-V_D(t)]$ and $\frac{d}{dt}(V_S(t)-V_D(t))$ at time $t \geq t_1$ implied by Equation (1.94).

The roots of characteristic equation corresponding to Equation (1.94) are,

$$k_{1,2}=-\frac{\lambda_P\lambda_D}{2}\pm\sqrt{\frac{\lambda_P^2\lambda_D^2}{4}-\lambda_P\lambda_{S2}} \tag{1.101}$$

Now I have to examine the behavior of $[V_S(t)-V_D(t)]$ for $t_0 \leq t < t_1$. I restrict myself to the *critically damped case* (see [19]) where $\frac{\lambda_P^2\lambda_D^2}{4}=\lambda_P\lambda_{S2}$. Other two cases ($\frac{\lambda_P^2\lambda_D^2}{4}>\lambda_P\lambda_{S2}$ and $\frac{\lambda_P^2\lambda_D^2}{4}<\lambda_P\lambda_{S2}$) require much more calculation efforts and provide similar results.

If $\frac{\lambda_P^2\lambda_D^2}{4}=\lambda_P\lambda_{S2}$ the solution of Equation (1.94) is,

$$V_S(t)-V_D(t)=(C_1+C_2(t-t_0))\exp\left\{-\frac{\lambda_P\lambda_D}{2}(t-t_0)\right\}, \tag{1.102}$$

where $C_1=0$ and $C_2=\delta$ are constants.

Therefore the final values here for Equation (1.94) at time $t=t_1$, that at the same time are initial values for Equation (1.100), are the following,

$$V_S(t_1)-V_D(t_1)=\delta(t_1-t_0)\exp\left\{-\frac{\lambda_P\lambda_D}{2}(t_1-t_0)\right\},$$

$$\frac{d}{dt}\left(V_S(t_1)-V_D(t_1)\right)=\delta\left[1-\frac{\lambda_P\lambda_D}{2}(t_1-t_0)\right]\exp\left\{-\frac{\lambda_P\lambda_D}{2}(t_1-t_0)\right\}.$$

The roots of characteristic equation corresponding to Equation (1.100) are,

$$k_{1,2}=-\frac{\lambda_P\lambda_D}{2}\pm\sqrt{\frac{\lambda_P^2\lambda_D^2}{4}-\lambda_P\left(\lambda_{S1}+\lambda_{S2}\right)} \tag{1.103}$$

To calculate the eventual share on the market for a stronger business entity it is sufficient to solve Equation (1.100) and use the following formula in the limit,

$$\frac{d^2V_{S1}(t)}{dt^2}=-\lambda_P\lambda_{S1}\left(V_S(t)-V_D(t)\right) \tag{1.104}$$

Since $\frac{\lambda_P^2\lambda_D^2}{4}=\lambda_P\lambda_{S2}$ then $\frac{\lambda_P^2\lambda_D^2}{4}<\lambda_P\left(\lambda_{S1}+\lambda_{S2}\right)$, and the solution of Equation (1.100) for $t\geq t_1$ is,

$$V_S(t)-V_D(t)=A\exp\left\{-\frac{\lambda_P\lambda_D}{2}(t-t_0)\right\}\sin\left(\sqrt{\lambda_P\left(\lambda_{S1}+\lambda_{S2}\right)-\frac{\lambda_P^2\lambda_D^2}{4}}\,(t-t_0)+\varphi_0\right), \tag{1.105}$$

where A and φ_0 are constants such as,

$$A\sin\left(\sqrt{\lambda_P\left(\lambda_{S1}+\lambda_{S2}\right)-\frac{\lambda_P^2\lambda_D^2}{4}}\,(t_1-t_0)+\varphi_0\right)=\delta\left(t_1-t_0\right),$$

$$A\sqrt{\lambda_P\left(\lambda_{S1}+\lambda_{S2}\right)-\frac{\lambda_P^2\lambda_D^2}{4}}\cos\left(\sqrt{\lambda_P\left(\lambda_{S1}+\lambda_{S2}\right)-\frac{\lambda_P^2\lambda_D^2}{4}}\,(t_1-t_0)+\varphi_0\right)=\delta.$$

Since $\frac{dV_{S1}(t_1)}{dt}=r_{S1}^0+\delta$ it takes place from Equation (1.104),

$$\frac{d^2V_{S1}(t)}{dt^2}=-\lambda_P\lambda_{S1}A\exp\left\{-\frac{\lambda_P\lambda_D}{2}(t-t_0)\right\}\sin\left(\sqrt{\lambda_P\left(\lambda_{S1}+\lambda_{S2}\right)-\frac{\lambda_P^2\lambda_D^2}{4}}\,(t-t_0)+\varphi_0\right) \tag{1.106}$$

$$\frac{dV_{S1}(t)}{dt} = \frac{\lambda_{S1}}{\lambda_{S1}+\lambda_{S2}} A \exp\left\{-\frac{\lambda_P \lambda_D}{2}(t-t_0)\right\}$$

$$\times \left[\begin{array}{l} \frac{\lambda_P \lambda_D}{2} \sin\left(\sqrt{\lambda_P(\lambda_{S1}+\lambda_{S2}) - \frac{\lambda_P^2 \lambda_D^2}{4}}(t-t_0)+\varphi_0\right) \\ +\sqrt{\lambda_P(\lambda_{S1}+\lambda_{S2}) - \frac{\lambda_P^2 \lambda_D^2}{4}} \cos\left(\sqrt{\lambda_P(\lambda_{S1}+\lambda_{S2}) - \frac{\lambda_P^2 \lambda_D^2}{4}}(t-t_0)+\varphi_0\right) \end{array} \right] + C_3 \tag{1.107}$$

where $C_3 = r_{S1}^0 + \delta - \frac{\lambda_{S1}}{\lambda_{S1}+\lambda_{S21}} \delta \left[1 + \frac{\lambda_P \lambda_D}{2}(t_1 - t_0)\right] \exp\left\{-\frac{\lambda_P \lambda_D}{2}(t_1 - t_0)\right\}$.

Thus it takes place for $t \to +\infty$,

$$\frac{dV_{S1}(t)}{dt} \to r_{S1}^0 + \delta - \frac{\lambda_{S1}}{\lambda_{S1}+\lambda_{S21}} \delta \left[1 + \frac{\lambda_P \lambda_D}{2}(t_1 - t_0)\right] \exp\left\{-\frac{\lambda_P \lambda_D}{2}(t_1 - t_0)\right\} \tag{1.108}$$

Therefore for $t_1 \to +\infty$ it takes place,

$$\frac{\lambda_{S1}}{\lambda_{S1}+\lambda_{S21}} \delta \left[1 + \frac{\lambda_P \lambda_D}{2}(t_1 - t_0)\right] \exp\left\{-\frac{\lambda_P \lambda_D}{2}(t_1 - t_0)\right\} \to 0, \tag{1.109}$$

and from there for $t \to +\infty$ and $t_1 \to +\infty$,

$$\frac{dV_{S1}(t)}{dt} \to r_{S1}^0 + \delta > r_{S1}^0 \tag{1.110}$$

As a result the inequality in Relation (1.110) shows that a stronger business entity, which can protractedly tolerate the product's price decline due to excessive product's supply on the market, eventually increases its share on the market for the product.

To calculate the eventual share on the market for a weaker business entity it is sufficient to use the following formula for $t_0 \le t < +\infty$,

$$\frac{d^2V_{S2}(t)}{dt^2} = -\lambda_P \lambda_{S2}\left(V_S(t) - V_D(t)\right) \tag{1.111}$$

To find $\frac{dV_{S2}(t_1)}{dt}$ I use Equation (1.102) and Equation (1.111) for $t_0 \le t < t_1$, and initial value $\frac{dV_{S2}(t_0)}{dt} = r_{S2}^0$,

$$\frac{d^2V_{S2}(t)}{dt^2} = -\lambda_P \lambda_{S2}\,\delta\,(t-t_0)\exp\left\{-\frac{\lambda_P\lambda_D}{2}(t-t_0)\right\}, \tag{1.112}$$

$$\frac{dV_{S2}(t)}{dt} = \frac{2\lambda_{S2}}{\lambda_D}\delta\left[(t-t_0)+\frac{2}{\lambda_P\lambda_D}\right]\exp\left\{-\frac{\lambda_P\lambda_D}{2}(t-t_0)\right\}+C_3, \tag{1.113}$$

where $C_3 = r_{S2}^0 - \delta$.

Therefore from Equation (1.113),

$$\frac{dV_{S2}(t_1)}{dt} = \frac{2\lambda_{S2}}{\lambda_D}\delta\left[(t_1-t_0)+\frac{2}{\lambda_P\lambda_D}\right]\exp\left\{-\frac{\lambda_P\lambda_D}{2}(t_1-t_0)\right\}+r_{S2}^0-\delta \tag{1.114}$$

Then it takes place from Equation (1.111) for $t_1 \le t < +\infty$,

$$\frac{d^2V_{S2}(t)}{dt^2} = -\lambda_P\lambda_{S2}\,A\exp\left\{-\frac{\lambda_P\lambda_D}{2}(t-t_0)\right\}\sin\left(\sqrt{\lambda_P(\lambda_{S1}+\lambda_{S2})-\frac{\lambda_P^2\lambda_D^2}{4}}\,(t-t_0)+\varphi_0\right) \tag{1.115}$$

$$\frac{dV_{S2}(t)}{dt} = \frac{\lambda_{S2}}{\lambda_{S1}+\lambda_{S2}}A\exp\left\{-\frac{\lambda_P\lambda_D}{2}(t-t_0)\right\}$$
$$\times\left[\begin{array}{l}\frac{\lambda_P\lambda_D}{2}\sin\left(\sqrt{\lambda_P(\lambda_{S1}+\lambda_{S2})-\frac{\lambda_P^2\lambda_D^2}{4}}\,(t-t_0)+\varphi_0\right)\\ +\sqrt{\lambda_P(\lambda_{S1}+\lambda_{S2})-\frac{\lambda_P^2\lambda_D^2}{4}}\cos\left(\sqrt{\lambda_P(\lambda_{S1}+\lambda_{S2})-\frac{\lambda_P^2\lambda_D^2}{4}}\,(t-t_0)+\varphi_0\right)\end{array}\right]+C_3 \tag{1.116}$$

where $C_3 = r_{S2}^0 - \delta - \frac{\lambda_{S2}}{\lambda_{S1}+\lambda_{S21}}\delta\left[1+\frac{\lambda_P\lambda_D}{2}(t_1-t_0)\right]\exp\left\{-\frac{\lambda_P\lambda_D}{2}(t_1-t_0)\right\}$.

Thus it takes place for $t \to +\infty$,

$$\frac{dV_{S2}(t)}{dt} \to r_{S2}^0 - \delta - \frac{\lambda_{S2}}{\lambda_{S1}+\lambda_{S21}}\delta\left[1+\frac{\lambda_P\lambda_D}{2}(t_1-t_0)\right]\exp\left\{-\frac{\lambda_P\lambda_D}{2}(t_1-t_0)\right\} \tag{1.117}$$

Therefore for $t_1 \to +\infty$ it takes place,

$$\frac{\lambda_{S2}}{\lambda_{S1}+\lambda_{S21}}\delta\left[1+\frac{\lambda_P\lambda_D}{2}(t_1-t_0)\right]\exp\left\{-\frac{\lambda_P\lambda_D}{2}(t_1-t_0)\right\} \to 0, \tag{1.118}$$

and from there for $t \to +\infty$ and $t_1 \to +\infty$,

$$\frac{dV_{S2}(t)}{dt} \to r_{S2}^0 - \delta < r_{S2}^0 \tag{1.119}$$

As a result the inequality in Relation (1.119) shows that a weaker business entity, which has to decrease the product's supply in order to ease the product's price decline due to excessive amount of product on the market, eventually loses its share on the market for the product.

Thus it takes place for the total product's supply on the market for $t \to +\infty$,

$$\frac{d}{dt}\left(V_{S1}(t)+V_{S2}(t)\right) \to \left(r_{S1}^0 + r_{S2}^0\right) - \delta\left[1+\frac{\lambda_P \lambda_D}{2}(t_1 - t_0)\right]\exp\left\{-\frac{\lambda_P \lambda_D}{2}(t_1 - t_0)\right\} \tag{1.120}$$

Therefore for $t_1 \to +\infty$ it takes place,

$$\delta\left[1+\frac{\lambda_P \lambda_D}{2}(t_1 - t_0)\right]\exp\left\{-\frac{\lambda_P \lambda_D}{2}(t_1 - t_0)\right\} \to 0, \tag{1.121}$$

and from there for $t \to +\infty$ and $t_1 \to +\infty$,

$$\frac{d}{dt}\left(V_{S1}(t)+V_{S2}(t)\right) \to r_D^0 = \left(r_{S1}^0 + r_{S2}^0\right) \tag{1.122}$$

Thus Relation (1.122) shows that result of prolonged excessive supply of the product to market is that at the limit total market for the product doesn't change while a stronger business entity increases the product's share, and a weaker business entity loses the product's share.

1.6 Inter-Industrial Dynamics

To describe the dynamics of inter-industrial processes, which happen in market economy, I resort to Input-Output model of Wassily Leontief (see [16], [17]).

1.6.1 Model Assumptions

Let me consider the model with n products, and denote $\overline{V}_D(t) \geq 0$ the non-negative vector of the products' demand on the market. Each non-negative component $[V_D(t)]_i \geq 0$ of the vector $\overline{V}_D(t) \geq 0$ represents the demand on the market for particular product $i = 1,\ldots,n$.

Similarly I denote $\overline{V}_S(t)\geq 0$ the non-negative vector of the products' supply on the market, where each non-negative component $\left[V_S(t)\right]_i \geq 0$ of the vector $\overline{V}_S(t)\geq 0$ represents the supply on the market for particular product $i = 1,\ldots,n$.

I also denote $\overline{P}_R(t)\geq 0$ a non-negative vector of the products' prices on the market, where each non-negative component $\left[P_R(t)\right]_i \geq 0$ of the vector $\overline{P}_R(t)\geq 0$ represents the price on the market for particular product $i = 1,\ldots,n$.

Now I introduce a non-negative square matrix A, which consists of non-negative elements $a_{ij} \geq 0$ showing the amount of product i needed to produce a unit of product j (see [16], [17]).

Now I am ready to make the following assumption.

Proposition 3 Market Equilibrium in Multi-Product Economy

The equilibrium on the market with multiple products is attained when demand for each product is equal to supply of the product minus the product's share used for other products' manufacturing.

Mathematically it means the following,

$$\left[V_D(t)\right]_i = \left[V_S(t)\right]_i - \sum_{j=1}^{n} a_{ij}\left[V_S(t)\right]_j \tag{1.123}$$

where $a_{ij} \geq 0$ and $i = 1,\ldots,n$.

Hence Equation (1.123) can be rewritten in the matrix form,

$$\overline{V}_D(t) = (I - A)\overline{V}_S(t) \tag{1.124}$$

where I is an identity matrix of size n.

It is known (see [2]) that for inverse matrix $(I - A)^{-1}$ to exist, and to be non-negative it is necessary and sufficient that Frobenius value (i.e. an eigenvalue that has maximum module) of non-negative matrix A be less than one.

I assume that the market had been in equilibrium position until time $t = t_0$; the volumes of products' supply $\overline{V}_S(t)$ and demand $\overline{V}_D(t)$ on market were described by Equation (1.124), and products' supply and demand both were developing with constant rates $\frac{d\overline{V}_D(t)}{dt} = \overline{r}_D^0$ and $\frac{d\overline{V}_S(t)}{dt} = \overline{r}_S^0$ linked by the following matrix equation,

$$\overline{r}_D^0 = (I - A)\overline{r}_S^0 \tag{1.125}$$

1.6.2 Fluctuations of Products' Supply and Demand

Now as an example I require that that at time $t = t_0$ there is a change in the vector of products' demand on the market with a constant vector of rates $\overline{\delta} \neq 0$,

$$\overline{r}_D(t) = \begin{cases} \overline{r}_D^0, & t < t_0 \\ \overline{r}_D^0 + \overline{\delta}, & t = t_0 \end{cases} \tag{1.126}$$

That event creates the products' shortage on the market, which starts building with the following rate $[(I - A)\overline{r}_S(t) - \overline{r}_D(t)]$, where $t \geq t_0$ and $(I - A)\overline{r}_S(t_0) - \overline{r}_D(t_0) = -\overline{\delta}$.

Here is the system of ordinary differential matrix equations connecting at each point in time the products' demand $V_D(t)$, the products' supply $V_S(t)$, and the products' prices $P_R(t)$,

$$\frac{d\overline{P}_R(t)}{dt} = -\Lambda_P [(I - A)\overline{V}_S(t) - \overline{V}_D(t)] \tag{1.127}$$

$$\frac{d^2\overline{V}_S(t)}{dt^2} = \Lambda_S \frac{d\overline{P}_R(t)}{dt} \tag{1.128}$$

$$\frac{d^2\overline{V}_D(t)}{dt^2} = -\Lambda_D \frac{d^2\overline{P}_R(t)}{dt^2} \tag{1.129}$$

where $t \geq t_0$ and Λ_S, Λ_D, Λ_P, –.diagonal matrices with non-negative constant elements $[\Lambda_S]_{ii} \geq 0$, $[\Lambda_D]_{ii} \geq 0$, $[\Lambda_P]_{ii} \geq 0$, respectively on the main diagonal.[1]

The preceding matrix Equations (1.127 – 129) can be replaced with the following second-order ordinary differential matrix equation about the vector of volumes of products' surpluses (or shortages) $\hat{V}(t) = [(I - A)\overline{V}_S(t) - \overline{V}_D(t)]$,

$$\frac{d^2\hat{V}(t)}{dt^2} + \Lambda_P \Lambda_D \frac{d\hat{V}(t)}{dt} + \Lambda_P \Lambda_S (I - A)\hat{V}(t) = \overline{0} \tag{1.130}$$

[1] It is worth to note that matrix Equations (1.127 – 129) mean that only supply of products for external needs is traded on the market, and participates in determination of products' prices. It implies that supply of products that is used during manufacturing processes is not traded on the market (e.g., products for manufacturing needs are supplied according to contracts outside of market but in agreement with prices determined by market for the external needs). A different approach is to trade all (or partial) supply of products on the market as was explored in [8].

where $\hat{V}(t_0) = \overline{0}$ and $\frac{d\hat{V}(t_0)}{dt} = -\overline{\delta}$.

Solution $\hat{V}(t)$ of matrix Equation (1.130) is sought in the way similar to the one I described earlier for the second-order ordinary differential equations in scalar form (see [1], [18]).

I introduce the vector $\overline{Y}(t)$ of size $2n$, where

$$\overline{Y}(t) = \begin{pmatrix} \frac{d\hat{V}(t)}{dt} & \hat{V}(t) \end{pmatrix}^T$$

and rewrite matrix Equation (1.130) in so-called *normal form*,

$$\frac{d\overline{Y}(t)}{dt} = \Gamma \overline{Y}(t) \tag{1.131}$$

where Γ is a square matrix of size $2n \times 2n$,

$$\Gamma = \begin{pmatrix} -\Lambda_P \Lambda_D & -\Lambda_P \Lambda_S (I - A) \\ I & 0 \end{pmatrix},$$

and initial conditions for vector $\overline{Y}(t)$ are,

$$\overline{Y}(t_0) = \begin{pmatrix} -\overline{\delta} & \overline{0} \end{pmatrix}^T.$$

The solution of matrix Equation (1.131) can be expressed in the matrix form for $t \geq t_0$ as,

$$\overline{Y}(t) = \overline{Y}(t_0) \exp\{\Gamma (t - t_0)\} \tag{1.132}$$

According to [20] the solution $\overline{Y}(t)$ of matrix Equation (1.132) is Lyapunov stable and asymptotically stable when each eigenvalue of matrix Γ has negative real part.

1.6.3 Fluctuations of Products' Prices

Now I will use the same example and look at the fluctuations of the products' prices.

At first I require that that at time $t = t_0$ there is a change in the vector of products' demand on the market with a constant vector of rates $\overline{\delta} \neq 0$,

$$\bar{r}_D(t) = \begin{cases} \bar{r}_D^0, & t < t_0 \\ \bar{r}_D^0 + \bar{\delta}, & t = t_0 \end{cases} \tag{1.133}$$

As earlier it creates the products' shortage on the market developing with the following rate $[(I-A)\bar{r}_S(t) - \bar{r}_D(t)]$, where $t \geq t_0$ and $(I-A)\bar{r}_S(t_0) - \bar{r}_D(t_0) = -\bar{\delta}$.

Here I can use the same system of matrix Equations (1.127 – 129) connecting at each point in time the products' demand $\bar{V}_D(t)$, the products' supply $\bar{V}_S(t)$, and the products' prices $\bar{P}_R(t)$.

I can differentiate matrix Equation (1.127), integrate matrix Equations (1.128 – 129), and receive the following system of ordinary differential matrix equations,

$$\frac{d^2\bar{P}_R(t)}{dt^2} = -\Lambda_P\left[(I-A)\frac{d\bar{V}_S(t)}{dt} - \frac{d\bar{V}_D(t)}{dt}\right] \tag{1.134}$$

$$\frac{d\bar{V}_S(t)}{dt} = \Lambda_S\,\bar{P}_R(t) + \bar{C}_1 \tag{1.135}$$

$$\frac{d\bar{V}_D(t)}{dt} = -\Lambda_D\frac{d\bar{P}_R(t)}{dt} + \bar{C}_2 \tag{1.136}$$

where $\bar{C}_1$ and $\bar{C}_2$ are vectors of integration's constants.

The preceding matrix Equations (1.134 – 136) can be replaced with the following second-order ordinary differential matrix equation about the products' prices $\bar{P}_R(t)$,

$$\frac{d^2\bar{P}_R(t)}{dt^2} + \Lambda_P\Lambda_D\frac{d\bar{P}_R(t)}{dt} + \Lambda_P(I-A)\Lambda_S\,\bar{P}_R(t) + \bar{C}_3 = 0 \tag{1.137}$$

where $\bar{C}_3 = \Lambda_P\left((I-A)\bar{C}_1 - \bar{C}_2\right)$ is a constant vector.

The constant vector $\bar{C}_3$ serves for reconciliation between vector of products' supply $\bar{V}_S(t)$ and vector of products' demand $\bar{V}_D(t)$, and vector of products' prices $\bar{P}_R(t)$ at initial time $t = t_0$.

I rewrite matrix Equation (1.137) using a variable $\bar{P}_1(t) = \bar{P}_R(t) + \Lambda_S^{-1}\left(\bar{C}_1 - (I-A)^{-1}\bar{C}_2\right)$,

$$\frac{d^2\bar{P}_1(t)}{dt^2} + \Lambda_P\Lambda_D\frac{d\bar{P}_1(t)}{dt} + \Lambda_P(I-A)\Lambda_S\,\bar{P}_1(t) = 0 \tag{1.138}$$

The initial conditions for $\overline{P}_R(t)$ are $\overline{P}_R(t_0) = \overline{P}_R^0$ and $\frac{d\overline{P}_R(t_0)}{dt} = \overline{0}$ from Equation (1.127).

Therefore the initial conditions for $\overline{P}_1(t)$ are $\overline{P}_1(t_0) = -\Lambda_S^{-1}(I - A)^{-1}\overline{\delta}$ and $\frac{d\overline{P}_1(t_0)}{dt} = \overline{0}$.

Again I introduce the vector $\overline{Z}(t)$ of size $2n$, where

$$\overline{Z}(t) = \begin{pmatrix} \frac{d\overline{P}_1(t)}{dt} & \overline{P}_1(t) \end{pmatrix}^T$$

and rewrite matrix Equation (1.138) into *normal form*,

$$\frac{d\overline{Z}(t)}{dt} = \mathrm{E}\overline{Z}(t) \tag{1.139}$$

where E is a square matrix of size $2n \times 2n$,

$$\mathrm{E} = \begin{pmatrix} -\Lambda_P \Lambda_D & -\Lambda_P (I - A)\Lambda_S \\ I & 0 \end{pmatrix},$$

and initial conditions for vector $\overline{Z}(t)$ are,

$$\overline{Z}(t_0) = \begin{pmatrix} \overline{0} & -\Lambda_S^{-1}(I - A)^{-1}\overline{\delta} \end{pmatrix}^T.$$

The solution of matrix Equation (1.139) can be expressed in the matrix form for $t \geq t_0$ as,

$$\overline{Z}(t) = \overline{Z}(t_0)\exp\{\mathrm{E}(t - t_0)\} \tag{1.140}$$

Once more the solution $\overline{Z}(t)$ of matrix Equation (1.140) is Lyapunov stable and asymptotically stable when each eigenvalue of matrix E has negative real part.

1.6.4 Discussion of Model Assumptions

The Input-Output model employed here is a linear model. It represents may be said a snapshot of economy where outputs' changes are linearly proportional to the inputs' changes for small changes of inputs (and for small changes in time).

If one wants to use that model for big changes of inputs or time she has to consider changes in technological processes showing for each product the amount of other products needed to produce a unit the product and represented by a matrix A. However the impact of these changes on the changes of outputs is not linear as will be shown in Chapter 3.

Another point to consider is that both Equation (1.123) and Equation (1.127) assume that shortages (surpluses) of products on the market $\hat{V}(t) = \left[(I - A)\overline{V}_S(t) - \overline{V}_D(t)\right]$ impact the products' prices. There are three players on the products' market. The first one is a group of the products' suppliers whose influence is represented by vector $\overline{V}_S(t)$. The second one is a group of the products' ultimate consumers whose influence is represented by vector $\overline{V}_D(t)$. The third one is a group of the products' industrial consumers whose influence is represented by vector $A\overline{V}_S(t)$. And the total influence of industrial suppliers and consumers is represented on market by vector $(I - A)\overline{V}_S(t)$. It means that at the same time industry instantly consumes some products on the market, processes them, and supplies output products back to the market. Since the presented model supposes that process of taking the system into another equilibrium state takes some time then noticeably model should also presume that between the time of products' consumption and time of supplying the products back to the market should be a timing lag necessary for industry to process the input products and produce the output products. Such assumption will not change the obtained results in the limit but it will change the path that system takes to approach to these results in the limit.

1.7 Summary

In the first Chapter I described the models, which were focusing on the processes that happen in real economy. I described how the shortages (surpluses) of products on the market drive the changes in the products' prices that in turn force the changes in the products' supply and demand.

In next Chapter I describe the models, which are focusing on the monetary aspects of economic systems. I introduce the monetary market, and also describe the markets for equities and derivatives.

Chapter 2

FINANCIAL MARKETS

2.1 INTRODUCTION

In this and the following Chapter I use material from the first Chapter. Based on that material I present more advanced models describing quite sophisticated economic phenomena.

Here in the second Chapter I focus on three topics related to finances.

At first I describe the mathematical model dealing with the nature of inflation and how the inflation is created. Then I present the model showing the functioning of monetary market and explain its connection with a real economy. Finally I introduce the model showing the functioning of stock market and demonstrate how equities and derivatives are priced there.

Originally material of this Chapter was mostly presented in [9], [12] – [15], [21].

2.2 INFLATION

2.2.1 Outline of Inflationary Phenomenon

At first I have to define inflation. For purpose of described here mathematical approach to economic dynamics I define *Inflation* as a non-cyclical (i.e. systematic) process of raising the products' prices.

According to material presented in the first Chapter the products' prices are raised when the demand for products exceeds the products' supply. I distinct two situations related to the rise of the products' prices, and describe them separately.

The first case is when the products' demand increases (or products' supply decreases) due to some occasional event, which causes the rise of the products' prices bringing an economic system to new equilibrium point.

The second case is when the products' demand constantly increases due to some systematic event such as pumping more money into economy. It causes the systematic rise of the products' prices but economic system never comes to new equilibrium point.

2.2.2 Occasional Rise of Products' Prices

Here again I consider an economical model with one product.

As earlier I assume that the market had been in equilibrium position until time $t = t_0$, the volumes of product's supply $V_S(t)$ and demand $V_D(t)$ on market were equal, and they both were developing with constant rate r_D^0.

$$V_D(t) = r_D^0 (t - t_0) + V_D^0 \tag{2.1}$$

$$V_S(t) = V_D(t) \tag{2.2}$$

where $V_D(t_0) = V_D^0$.

Then at time $t = t_0$ the product's demand is increased on the amount $\Delta > 0$,

$$V_D(t) = \begin{cases} V_D^0, & (t - t_0) \to -0 \\ V_D^0 + \Delta, & t = t_0 \end{cases} \tag{2.3}$$

That event creates the product's shortage on the market $V_S(t_0) - V_D(t_0) = -\Delta$.

Now I can write the system of ordinary differential equations connecting at each point in time the product's demand $V_D(t)$, the product's supply $V_S(t)$, and the product's price $P_R(t)$,

$$\frac{dP_R(t)}{dt} = -\lambda_P \left(V_S(t) - V_D(t)\right) \tag{2.4}$$

$$\frac{d^2 V_S(t)}{dt^2} = \lambda_S \frac{dP_R(t)}{dt} \tag{2.5}$$

$$\frac{d^2 V_D(t)}{dt^2} = -\lambda_D \frac{d^2 P_R(t)}{dt^2} \tag{2.6}$$

where $t > t_0$.

Initial conditions for the product's price $P_R(t)$ are $P_R(t_0) = P_R^0$ and $\frac{dP_R(t_0)}{dt} = \lambda_P \Delta$.

Let me differentiate Equation (2.4) and integrate both Equation (2.5) and Equation (2.6),

$$\frac{d^2P_R(t)}{dt^2} = -\lambda_P \frac{d}{dt}\left(V_S(t) - V_D(t)\right) \tag{2.7}$$

$$\frac{dV_S(t)}{dt} - \lambda_S P_R(t) + C_1 \tag{2.8}$$

$$\frac{dV_D(t)}{dt} = -\lambda_D \frac{dP_R(t)}{dt} + C_2 \tag{2.9}$$

where $C_1 = r_D^0 - \lambda_S P_R^0$ and $C_2 = r_D^0 + \lambda_P \lambda_D \Delta$ are integration's constants.

Thus I can obtain the following second-order ordinary differential equation about the product's price $P_R(t)$,

$$\frac{d^2P_R(t)}{dt^2} + \lambda_P \lambda_D \frac{dP_R(t)}{dt} + \lambda_P \lambda_S P_R(t) + C_3 = 0 \tag{2.10}$$

where $C_3 = -\lambda_P\left(\lambda_P \lambda_D \Delta + \lambda_S P_R^0\right)$ is a constant.

If I use new variable $P_1(t) = P_R(t) - P_R^0 - \frac{\lambda_P \lambda_D}{\lambda_S}\Delta$, the Equation (2.10) becomes,

$$\frac{d^2P_1(t)}{dt^2} + \lambda_P \lambda_D \frac{dP_1(t)}{dt} + \lambda_P \lambda_S P_1(t) = 0 \tag{2.11}$$

Therefore the initial conditions for $P_1(t)$ are $P_1(t_0) = -\frac{\lambda_P \lambda_D}{\lambda_S}\Delta$ and $\frac{dP_1(t_0)}{dt} = \lambda_P \Delta$.

The roots of characteristic equation corresponding to Equation (2.11) are,

$$k_{1,2} = -\frac{\lambda_P \lambda_D}{2} \pm \sqrt{\frac{\lambda_P^2 \lambda_D^2}{4} - \lambda_P \lambda_S} \tag{2.12}$$

(a) If $\frac{\lambda_P^2 \lambda_D^2}{4} > \lambda_P \lambda_S$ the solution of Equation (2.11) is,

$$P_1(t) = C_1 \exp\{k_1 (t - t_0)\} + C_2 \exp\{k_2 (t - t_0)\}, \tag{2.13}$$

where C_1 and C_2 are constants.

Since both $k_1 < 0$ and $k_2 < 0$ it takes place $P_1(t) \to 0$ for $t \to +\infty$.

(b) If $\frac{\lambda_P^2 \lambda_D^2}{4} = \lambda_P \lambda_S$ the solution of Equation (2.11) is,

$$P_1(t) = \left(C_1 + C_2 (t - t_0)\right) \exp\left\{ -\frac{\lambda_P \lambda_D}{2} (t - t_0) \right\}, \tag{2.14}$$

where C_1 and C_2 are constants.

Since $\lambda_P \lambda_D > 0$ it takes place $P_1(t) \to 0$ for $t \to +\infty$.

(c) If $\frac{\lambda_P^2 \lambda_D^2}{4} < \lambda_P \lambda_S$ the solution of Equation (2.11) is,

$$P_1(t) = \exp\left\{ -\frac{\lambda_P \lambda_D}{2} (t - t_0) \right\}$$

$$\times \left(C_1 \cos\left(\sqrt{\lambda_P \lambda_S - \frac{\lambda_P^2 \lambda_D^2}{4}} (t - t_0) \right) + C_2 \sin\left(\sqrt{\lambda_P \lambda_S - \frac{\lambda_P^2 \lambda_D^2}{4}} (t - t_0) \right) \right) \tag{2.15}$$

where C_1 and C_2 are constants.

Since $\lambda_P \lambda_D > 0$ it takes place $P_1(t) \to 0$ for $t \to +\infty$, and I have covered all possible cases.

Hence since $P_1(t) \to 0$ for $t \to +\infty$ then it takes place $P_R(t) \to \left(P_R^0 + \frac{\lambda_P \lambda_D}{\lambda_S} \Delta \right) > P_R^0$ for $t \to +\infty$.

Thus in the limit the product's price has increased and has stabilized as a result of initial rise in the product's demand.

2.2.3 Systematic Rise of Products' Prices

Again I consider a model with one product.

As earlier the market had been in equilibrium position until time $t = t_0$, the volumes of product's supply $V_S(t)$ and demand $V_D(t)$ on market were equal, and they both were developing with constant rate r_D^0.

$$V_D(t) = r_D^0 (t - t_0) + V_D^0 \tag{2.16}$$

$$V_S(t) = V_D(t) \tag{2.17}$$

Then at time $t = t_0$ the rate of product's demand starts accelerating by increasing with an amount $\varepsilon > 0$ in the unit time, i.e. the authority has started to pump money into economic system with a constant rate,

$$\frac{d^2 V_D(t)}{dt^2} = \begin{cases} 0, & t < t_0 \\ \varepsilon, & t \geq t_0 \end{cases} \tag{2.18}$$

That event creates the product's shortage on the market, which starts building with the following rate $[r_S(t) - r_D(t)]$, where $r_D(t_0) = r_D^0 + \varepsilon(t - t_0)$ and $t \geq t_0$.

But there is also usual negative impact of the raising prices on the product's demand. How to account for both the positive impact of money's pumping to economic system and the negative impact of raising prices in the model?

The answer gives the following assumption for dynamics of multiple demand forces.

Hypothesis 6 Behavior of Multiple Demand Forces

When there are multiple "demand forces" acting on the market, their impacts are summed.

Now I can write the system of ordinary differential equations connecting at each point in time the product's demand $V_D(t)$, the product's supply $V_S(t)$, and the product's price $P_R(t)$,

$$\frac{dP_R(t)}{dt} = -\lambda_P \left(V_S(t) - V_D(t)\right) \tag{2.19}$$

$$\frac{d^2 V_S(t)}{dt^2} = \lambda_S \frac{dP_R(t)}{dt} \tag{2.20}$$

$$\frac{d^2 V_D(t)}{dt^2} = \varepsilon - \lambda_D \frac{d^2 P_R(t)}{dt^2} \tag{2.21}$$

where $t > t_0$.

Initial conditions for the product's price $P_R(t)$ are $P_R(t_0) = P_R^0$ and $\frac{dP_R(t_0)}{dt} = 0$.

Let me differentiate Equation (2.19) and integrate both Equation (2.20) and Equation (2.21),

$$\frac{d^2 P_R(t)}{dt^2} = -\lambda_P \frac{d}{dt}\left(V_S(t) - V_D(t)\right) \tag{2.22}$$

$$\frac{dV_S(t)}{dt} = \lambda_S P_R(t) + C_1 \tag{2.23}$$

$$\frac{dV_D(t)}{dt} = \varepsilon(t - t_0) - \lambda_D \frac{dP_R(t)}{dt} + C_2 \tag{2.24}$$

where $C_1 = r_D^0 - \lambda_S P_R^0$ and $C_2 = r_D^0$ are integration's constants.

Thus I can obtain the following second-order ordinary differential equation about the product's price $P_R(t)$,

$$\frac{d^2 P_R(t)}{dt^2} + \lambda_P \lambda_D \frac{dP_R(t)}{dt} + \lambda_P \lambda_S P_R(t) - \lambda_P \varepsilon(t - t_0) - \lambda_P \lambda_S P_R^0 = 0 \tag{2.25}$$

If I use new variable $P_1(t) = P_R(t) - \frac{1}{\lambda_S}\varepsilon(t - t_0) - \left(P_R^0 - \frac{\lambda_D}{\lambda_S^2}\varepsilon \right)$, the Equation (2.25) becomes,

$$\frac{d^2 P_1(t)}{dt^2} + \lambda_P \lambda_D \frac{dP_1(t)}{dt} + \lambda_P \lambda_S P_1(t) = 0 \tag{2.26}$$

Therefore the initial conditions for $P_1(t)$ are $P_1(t_0) = \frac{\lambda_D}{\lambda_S^2}\varepsilon$ and $\frac{dP_1(t_0)}{dt} = -\frac{1}{\lambda_S}\varepsilon$.

The roots of characteristic equation corresponding to Equation (2.26) are,

$$k_{1,2} = -\frac{\lambda_P \lambda_D}{2} \pm \sqrt{\frac{\lambda_P^2 \lambda_D^2}{4} - \lambda_P \lambda_S} \tag{2.27}$$

(a) If $\frac{\lambda_P^2 \lambda_D^2}{4} > \lambda_P \lambda_S$ the solution of Equation (2.26) is,

$$P_1(t) = C_1 \exp\{k_1 (t - t_0)\} + C_2 \exp\{k_2 (t - t_0)\}, \tag{2.28}$$

where C_1 and C_2 are constants.

Since both $k_1 < 0$ and $k_2 < 0$ it takes place $P_1(t) \to 0$ for $t \to +\infty$.

(b) If $\frac{\lambda_P^2 \lambda_D^2}{4} = \lambda_P \lambda_S$ the solution of Equation (2.26) is,

$$P_1(t) = (C_1 + C_2(t - t_0))\exp\left\{-\frac{\lambda_P \lambda_D}{2}(t - t_0)\right\}, \tag{2.29}$$

where C_1 and C_2 are constants.

Since $\lambda_P \lambda_D > 0$ it takes place $P_1(t) \to 0$ for $t \to +\infty$.

(c) If $\frac{\lambda_P^2 \lambda_D^2}{4} < \lambda_P \lambda_S$ the solution of Equation (2.26) is,

$$P_1(t) = \exp\left\{-\frac{\lambda_P \lambda_D}{2}(t - t_0)\right\}$$

$$\times\left(C_1 \cos\left(\sqrt{\lambda_P \lambda_S - \frac{\lambda_P^2 \lambda_D^2}{4}}(t - t_0)\right) + C_2 \sin\left(\sqrt{\lambda_P \lambda_S - \frac{\lambda_P^2 \lambda_D^2}{4}}(t - t_0)\right)\right) \tag{2.30}$$

where C_1 and C_2 are constants.

Since $\lambda_P \lambda_D > 0$ it takes place $P_1(t) \to 0$ for $t \to +\infty$, and I have covered all possible cases.

Since $P_1(t) \to 0$ for $t \to +\infty$ it takes place $P_R(t) \to \frac{1}{\lambda_S}\varepsilon(t - t_0) + \left(P_R^0 - \frac{\lambda_D}{\lambda_S^2}\varepsilon\right)$ for $t \to +\infty$.

Thus if the rate of the product's demand is constantly increasing (due to pumping more money into economic system), the product's price has also been constantly increasing with rate proportional to the changes in rate of the product's demand. The economic system never comes to new equilibrium point where product's demand and supply becomes equal.

2.3 Money Market

2.3.1 Significance of Money Market

The role of monetary market is very significant in economic system.

At first, the monetary market serves to balance the demand and supply of peculiar product called *money*. The indicator of equilibrium on the monetary market is the price of money called an *interest rate*. I won't describe here the nature of interest rates; I postpone it until Chapter 3.

Secondly, other regular products are traded in economic system not directly but the exchange is mediated with a help of money. And these perpetual exchanges also affect the monetary market.

Here I present the model describing the monetary market itself and its connections with real economy and other markets for ordinary products.

2.3.2 Money Market's Dynamics

Analogously to the regular products' market, I assume that when money's supply and the one's demand are equal, the monetary market lies in an equilibrium position. It means that the money's supply and demand are both developing with a constant rate and the price of money is fixed. The price of money is universally represented by an interest rate.

When such balance between the money's supply and demand is broken, the money's market is experienced the economic forces, which act to bring the market to a new equilibrium position.

These market forces are described by the following ordinary differential equations regarding to the money's supply $M_S(t)$, demand $M_D(t)$, and price $P_M(t)$,

$$\frac{dP_M(t)}{dt} = -\mu_P \cdot (M_S(t) - M_D(t)) \tag{2.31}$$

$$\frac{d^2 M_S(t)}{dt^2} = \mu_S \cdot \frac{dP_M(t)}{dt} \tag{2.32}$$

$$\frac{d^2 M_D(t)}{dt^2} = -\mu_D \cdot \frac{d^2 P_M(t)}{dt^2} \tag{2.33}$$

In Equations (2.31 – 33) above the values $\mu_P, \mu_S, \mu_D \geq 0$ are constants.

The meaning of Equations (2.31 – 33) is as follows.

I call the negative difference between the money's supply and the one's demand at each point in time as *a money shortage*. Likewise I call *a money surplus* at the same time the positive difference between the money's supply and demand. As I said earlier when the money's demand and supply are equal, the monetary market lies at the equilibrium position.

In situation when the money's demand and supply are not equal, the price of money experiences changes. As it was said earlier the price of money is expressed through the interest rate. If the money's supply exceeds the one's demand on monetary market, the price of money goes down, and it goes up in another circumstances. The rate of changes in the money's price at each point in time is developing with a pace inversely-linearly proportional to the money's shortage (or surplus) at the same time.

When the price of money changes, the money's supply undergoes changes. Equally when the price of money increases, the money's supply goes up, and it goes down in another circumstances. An acceleration (or deceleration) of the changes in the money's supply at each point in time is linearly proportional to the rate of changes in the money's price at the same time.

Also when the money's price changes, the money's demand experiences the oppressive effect. When the price of money increases, the money's demand goes down, and it goes up in another circumstances. An acceleration (or deceleration) of the changes in the money's demand at each point in time is inversely-linearly proportional to the acceleration (or deceleration) of changes in the money's price at the same time.

2.3.3 Relation between Markets of Money and Products

In this section I describe relationships that exist in economical system consisting of the single product's market and the monetary market.

I assume that at the beginning the product's supply and demand are equal, i.e. the product's market remains in an equilibrium position. Also the money's supply and demand are equal, and the monetary market remains in an equilibrium position as well.

a) Considering a scenario when the demand for money has been changed.

The increase of demand for money creates a growth in the price of money (an interest rate) and causes inflow of the money's supply. The inflow of money's supply increases the demand for product, which causes a growth in the product's price, and hence an increase of the product's supply.

The decrease of demand for money creates a reduction in the price of money (an interest rate) and causes outflow of the money's supply. The outflow of money's supply decreases the demand for product, which causes a reduction in the product's price, and hence a decrease of the product's supply.

b) Considering a scenario when the price of money has been changed.

A growth in the price of money (an interest rate) causes inflow of the money's supply. It increases the demand for product, which causes a growth in the product's price, and hence an increase of the product's supply.

A reduction in the price of money (an interest rate) causes outflow of the money's supply. It decreases the demand for product, which causes a reduction in the product's price, and hence a decrease of the product's supply.

c) Considering a scenario when the supply of money has been changed.

The increase of money's supply increases the demand for product, which causes a growth in the product's price, and therefore an increase of the product's supply.

The decrease of money's supply decreases the demand for product, which causes a reduction in the product's price, and therefore a decrease of the product's supply.

d) Considering a scenario when the product's price has been changed.

A growth in the product's price increases the product's supply.

A reduction in the product's price decreases the product's supply.

e) Considering a scenario when the product's supply has been changed.

That scenario is trivial.

2.3.4 Joined Markets for Money and Single Product

In this section I investigate in depth the scenario (a) from the previous section describing how changes on the monetary market impose the changes in the product's market. For this purpose I am going to operate with the model consisting of the market of single product and the monetary market.

At first I need to formalize the forenamed scenario through economic forces described by the ordinary differential equations.

The demand for product V_D and the product's supply V_S are equal until $t \le t_0$ and $V_D(t_0) = V_S(t_0) = V_D^0$. Therefore it holds $\frac{dV_D(t)}{dt} = \frac{dV_S(t)}{dt} = r_D^0$ until $t \le t_0$ where $r_D^0 \ge 0$ is a constant. The product's price is fixed $P_R(t) = P_R^0$ for $t \le t_0$.

Money's demand M_D and supply M_S are equal initially i.e. $M_D(t_0) = M_S(t_0) = M_D^0$. Therefore it holds $\frac{dM_D(t)}{dt} = \frac{dM_S(t)}{dt} = m_D^0$ until $t \le t_0$ where $m_D^0 \ge 0$ is a constant. The price of money (interest rate) is fixed $P_M(t) = P_M^0$ for $t \le t_0$.

I assume that the product's market and money's market are initially stationary relative to each other, i.e. it takes place $r_D^0 = m_D^0$ for $t \le t_0$.

According to scenario (a) at time $t = t_0$ I have the following conditions for monetary market $M_D(t_0) = M_0 + \Delta$, $M_S(t_0) = M_0$, $P_M(t_0) = P_M^0$ where $\Delta \ne 0$.

Therefore the deviation $[M_S(t_0) - M_D(t_0)]$ between the money's supply $M_S(t)$ and the money's demand $M_D(t)$ at time $t = t_0$ creates the economic forces for $t > t_0$, which are described by the following second-order linear homogeneous ordinary differential equation with constant coefficients,

$$\frac{d^2(M_S(t) - M_D(t))}{dt^2} + \mu_P\,\mu_D \frac{d(M_S(t) - M_D(t))}{dt} + \mu_P\,\mu_S\,(M_S(t) - M_D(t)) = 0 \tag{2.34}$$

Solution of Equation (2.34) depends on the roots of the corresponding characteristic equation depicted below,

$$k_{1,2} = -\frac{\mu_P\,\mu_D}{2} \pm \sqrt{\frac{\mu_P^2\,\mu_D^2}{4} - \mu_P\,\mu_S} \tag{2.35}$$

It is known from the theory of ordinary differential equations (for example, see [19]) that the solution of Equation (2.34) is different in the following situations: (a) the roots of characteristic equation are real and different $k_1 \ne k_2$, (b) the roots of characteristic equation are real and equal $k_1 = k_2$, and (c) the roots of characteristic equation are complex.

I describe here briefly what happened with deviation $[M_S(t) - M_D(t)]$ on the monetary market in the mentioned above situations.

In case of $\frac{\mu_P^2 \mu_D^2}{4} \geq \mu_P \mu_S$ the roots of characteristic equation are real. Here the money supply $M_S(t)$ asymptotically approaches the money demand $M_D(t)$ in the exponential-like manner. In case of $\frac{\mu_P^2 \mu_D^2}{4} < \mu_P \mu_S$ the roots of characteristic equation are complex. In this situation the money supply $M_S(t)$ asymptotically approaches the money demand $M_D(t)$ in the damped-oscillations-like manner.

In circumstances when the money's supply changes, it causes the changes in the demand for product on the market. Let me look at the correlation between the money's supply $M_S(t)$ and the demand $V_D(t)$ for product in the model. Here in the model with single product the whole money's supply has no other direction but to the market of single product.

I generalize aforesaid into the following statement.

Proposition 4 Relations between Money's Supply and Products' Demand

When money supply flows from the money market into market for products it is forming there the demand for products.

Mathematically it means the following integrating condition for the money's market and product's market in the portrayed model,

$$M_S(t) = V_D(t) \tag{2.36}$$

Therefore if the solution for the money supply $M_S(t)$ or demand for product $V_D(t)$ is placed into differential equation describing the product's supply $V_S(t)$, it will be obtained the second-order linear nonhomogeneous ordinary differential equation with constants coefficients describing the product's supply $V_S(t)$ for $t \geq t_0$. It is known (for example, see [18], [19]) that general solution of such nonhomogeneous equation represents the sum of the particular solution of the nonhomogeneous ordinary differential equation in question and the general solution of the corresponding homogeneous ordinary differential equation.

In the next section I produce the solution for such model.

2.3.5 Model of Joined Markets with Unilateral Relations

In this section I describe an illustrative example, showing how the equilibrium forces can be represented as the superposition of two sinusoids.

Consider the following example where at time $t = t_0$ there are the following conditions for the monetary market $\frac{dM_D(t_0)}{dt} = \frac{dM_S(t_0)}{dt} = m_D^0 = 0$, $M_D(t_0) = \Delta$, $M_S(t_0) = 0$, and $\Delta \neq 0$.

Let me assume in this example for simplicity that $\mu_D = 0$. Then from Equations (2.31 – 33) the second-order ordinary differential equation describing the money's supply $M_S(t)$ is as following,

$$\frac{d^2 M_S(t)}{dt^2} + \mu_P \mu_S \left(M_S(t) - M_D(t)\right) = 0 \tag{2.37}$$

or since $\frac{d^2 M_D(t)}{dt^2} = 0$, it is the same as,

$$\frac{d^2 \left(M_S(t) - M_D(t)\right)}{dt^2} + \mu_P \mu_S \left(M_S(t) - M_D(t)\right) = 0 \tag{2.38}$$

where $M_S(t_0) - M_D(t_0) = -\Delta$, and $\frac{d\left(M_S(t_0) - M_D(t_0)\right)}{dt} = 0$.

Therefore the solution of Equation (2.38) is

$$M_S(t) - M_D(t) = -\Delta \cdot \cos\left(\sqrt{\mu_P \mu_S}\,(t - t_0)\right) \tag{2.39}$$

and correspondingly

$$M_S(t) = -\Delta \cdot \cos\left(\sqrt{\mu_P \mu_S}\,(t - t_0)\right) + \Delta \tag{2.40}$$

At the same time $t = t_0$ I assume the following boundary conditions for the product's market $\frac{dV_D(t_0)}{dt} = \frac{dV_S(t_0)}{dt} = r_D^0$, $V_D(t_0) = V_S(t_0) = V_D^0$, $P_R(t_0) = P_R^0$ where $r_D^0 \geq 0$ and the following integrating condition connecting both the money's and the product's markets $M_S(t) = V_D(t)$.

Since $M_S(t) = V_D(t)$ it follows that $V_D^0 = M_S(t_0) = 0$ and $r_D^0 = m_D^0 = 0$.

Because the demand for product $V_D(t)$ here is only driven by the money's supply $M_S(t)$ without any feedback then it takes place for the coefficient $\lambda_D = 0$ (see Chapter 1). Thus from Equations (1.26 – 28) the second-order ordinary differential equation describing the product's supply $V_S(t)$ is as following,

$$\frac{d^2 V_S(t)}{dt^2} + \lambda_P \lambda_S \left(V_S(t) - M_S(t)\right) = 0 \tag{2.41}$$

where $V_S(t_0)=0$ and $\dfrac{dV_S(t_0)}{dt}=0$.

Consequently from [18] the solution of Equation (2.41) is,

$$V_S(t)=\Delta\left[\frac{\mu_P\,\mu_S}{\lambda_P\,\lambda_S-\mu_P\,\mu_S}\cos\left(\sqrt{\lambda_P\,\lambda_S}\,(t-t_0)\right)-\frac{\lambda_P\,\lambda_S}{\lambda_P\,\lambda_S-\mu_P\,\mu_S}\cos\left(\sqrt{\mu_P\,\mu_S}\,(t-t_0)\right)+1\right] \tag{2.42}$$

As it can be seen the solution of an illustrative example studied in this section and represented by Equation (2.42) corresponds to the sum of two sinusoid-like functions.

2.3.6 Model of Joined Markets with Bilateral Relations

In this section I describe an integrated model of the monetary market and the market of single product. To do so let me combine Equations (1.26 – 28) and (2.31 – 33) into one integrated system of ordinary differential equations using the integrating condition $M_S(t)=V_D(t)$,

$$\frac{dP_R(t)}{dt}=-\lambda_P\left(V_S(t)-M_S(t)\right) \tag{2.43}$$

$$\frac{dP_M(t)}{dt}=-\mu_P\left(M_S(t)-M_D(t)\right) \tag{2.44}$$

$$\frac{d^2V_S(t)}{dt^2}=\lambda_S\frac{dP_R(t)}{dt} \tag{2.45}$$

$$\frac{d^2M_S(t)}{dt^2}=\mu_S\frac{dP_M(t)}{dt}-\lambda_D\frac{d^2P_R(t)}{dt^2} \tag{2.46}$$

$$\frac{d^2M_D(t)}{dt^2}=-\mu_D\frac{d^2P_M(t)}{dt^2} \tag{2.47}$$

I can rewrite System (2.43 – 47) into following system of ordinary differential equations,

$$\frac{d^2\left(V_S(t)-M_S(t)\right)}{dt^2}+\lambda_P\lambda_D\frac{d(V_S(t)-M_S(t))}{dt}$$

$$+\lambda_P\lambda_S(V_S(t)-M_S(t))=\mu_P\mu_S(M_S(t)-M_D(t)) \tag{2.48}$$

$$\frac{d^2\left(M_S(t)-M_D(t)\right)}{dt^2}+\mu_P\mu_D\,\frac{d(M_S(t)-M_D(t))}{dt}$$

$$+\,\mu_P\mu_S(M_S(t)-M_D(t))=\lambda_P\lambda_D\,\frac{(V_S(t)-M_S(t))}{dt} \tag{2.49}$$

According to [18], [19] let me replace $\left(V_S(t)-M_S(t)\right)=\alpha\exp\{k\,t\}$ and $\left(M_S(t)-M_D(t)\right)=\beta\exp\{k\,t\}$ in order to reproduce System (2.48 – 49) as follows

$$\left(k^2+\lambda_P\,\lambda_D\,k+\lambda_P\,\lambda_S\right)\alpha-\mu_P\,\mu_S\,\beta=0 \tag{2.50}$$

$$-\lambda_P\,\lambda_D\,k\,\alpha+\left(k^2+\mu_P\,\mu_D\,k+\mu_P\,\mu_S\right)\beta=0 \tag{2.51}$$

To solve System (2.48 – 49) one looks for the roots of characteristic equation,

$$\begin{vmatrix}\left(k^2+\lambda_P\,\lambda_D\,k+\lambda_P\,\lambda_S\right) & -\mu_P\,\mu_S\\ -\lambda_P\,\lambda_D\,k & \left(k^2+\mu_P\,\mu_D\,k+\mu_P\,\mu_S\right)\end{vmatrix}=0\;, \tag{2.52}$$

then determines α and β from System (2.50 – 51), and finds the general solutions for $\left[V_S(t)-M_S(t)\right]$ and $\left[M_S(t)-M_D(t)\right]$ as a linear combination of corresponding particular solutions in accordance with [18], [19].

2.3.7 Intra-Industrial Dynamics in Joined Markets – Money and Single Product

In this section, as in the section 1.5 of Chapter 1, I consider the model where multiple suppliers provide the single product, and explore the impact the monetary market introduces to this situation.

At the beginning I assume that initially the total supply of the product and demand for it are equal, and the product's market remains in an equilibrium position. Also I assume that the money's supply and demand are equal, and the money's market is in an equilibrium position as well.

a) Considering case when the product's supply by one of the suppliers has changed.

The increase of the product's supply by one of the suppliers creates a reduction of the product's price. The first result of the product's price drop is the decrease of product's supply by the other suppliers. Another result of the product's price drop is an increase of the demand for product, which causes respectively the inflow of the money's supply, a growth in the price of money (an interest rate), and a decrease of the demand for money.

The decrease of the product's supply by one of the suppliers creates a growth of the product's price. The first result of the product's price advance is the increase of product's supply by the other suppliers. Another result of the product's price advance is a decrease of the demand for product, which causes respectively the outflow of the money's supply, a reduction in the price of money (an interest rate), and an increase of the demand for money.

b) Considering case when the product's price has changed.

A growth of the product's price increases the product's supply by the other suppliers and decreases the demand for product. The decrease in the demand for product respectively causes the outflow of the money's supply, a reduction in the price of money (an interest rate), and an increase of demand for money.

A reduction of the product's price decreases the product's supply by the other suppliers and increases the demand for product. The increase in the demand for product respectively causes the inflow of the money's supply, a growth in the price of money (an interest rate), and a decrease of demand for money.

c) Considering case when the supply of money has changed.

The inflow of money's supply causes a growth in the price of money (an interest rate), and a decrease of demand for money.

The outflow of money's supply causes a reduction in the price of money (an interest rate), and an increase of demand for money.

d) Considering case when the price of money (an interest rate) has changed.

A growth in the price of money (an interest rate) causes the decrease of demand for money.

A reduction in the price of money (an interest rate) causes the increase of demand for money.

e) Considering case when the demand for money has changed.

That scenario is trivial.

Now as in the first Chapter for illustrative purpose I consider the model, where two different suppliers are supplying a single product in the amounts $V_{S1}(t)$ and $V_{S2}(t)$ respectively on the market, and write the system of ordinary differential equations, which describes the economic forces acting both on the product's and on the monetary markets,

$$\frac{dP_R(t)}{dt} = -\lambda_P \left(V_S(t) - M_S(t)\right) \tag{2.53}$$

$$\frac{dP_M(t)}{dt} = -\mu_P \left(M_S(t) - M_D(t)\right) \tag{2.54}$$

$$V_S(t) = V_{S1}(t) + V_{S2}(t) \tag{2.55}$$

$$\frac{d^2 V_{S1}(t)}{dt^2} = \lambda_{S1} \frac{dP_R(t)}{dt} \tag{2.56}$$

$$\frac{d^2 V_{S2}(t)}{dt^2} = \lambda_{S2} \frac{dP_R(t)}{dt} \tag{2.57}$$

$$\frac{d^2M_S(t)}{dt^2} = \mu_S \frac{dP_M(t)}{dt} - \lambda_D \frac{d^2P_R(t)}{dt^2} \tag{2.58}$$

$$\frac{d^2M_D(t)}{dt^2} = -\mu_D \frac{d^2P_M(t)}{dt^2} \tag{2.59}$$

where both values $\lambda_{S1} \geq 0$ and $\lambda_{S2} \geq 0$ are constants.

I can generalize results on arbitrary number of suppliers providing product in the amount,

$$V_S(t) = V_{S1}(t) + V_{S2}(t) + \cdots + V_{Sm}(t) = \sum_{i=1}^{m} V_{Si}(t) \tag{2.60}$$

and rewrite System (2.53 – 59) into the following one,

$$\frac{d^2(V_S(t) - M_S(t))}{dt^2} + \lambda_P \lambda_D \frac{d(V_S(t) - M_S(t))}{dt}$$

$$+ \lambda_P \sum_{i=1}^{m} \lambda_{Si} (V_S(t) - M_S(t)) = \mu_P \mu_S (M_S(t) - M_D(t)) \tag{2.61}$$

$$\frac{d^2(M_S(t) - M_D(t))}{dt^2} + \mu_P \mu_D \frac{d(M_S(t) - M_D(t))}{dt}$$

$$+ \mu_P \mu_S (M_S(t) - M_D(t)) = \lambda_P \lambda_D \frac{(V_S(t) - M_S(t))}{dt} \tag{2.62}$$

where all values $\lambda_{Si} \geq 0$ are constants, and $m \geq 1$ is the number of suppliers.

2.3.8 Inter-Industrial Dynamics in Joined Markets – Money and Multiple Product

In this section I describe an integrated model of monetary and products' markets where multiple products are provided by multiple suppliers. The exposition presented here follows the approach outlined in the section 1.6 of Chapter 1.

I consider dynamics of integrated monetary and products' markets where the products' market includes numerous distinct products, each one of these products is provided by a single supplier, and the these products are related to each other through Input-Output model of Wassily Leontief (see [16], [17]).

Therefore following [16], [17] I introduce a square matrix A of size $n \times n$, which consists of elements $a_{ij} \geq 0$ expressing an amount of each product i needed for the production of one unit of a product j, and $n \geq 1$ is the number of products.

For the purpose of convenience in order to operate with multiple products I will work with vector notation. I denote $\overline{V}_S(t) \geq 0$ a non-negative vector of the products' supply on the market, where each non-negative component $[V_S(t)]_i \geq 0$ of the vector $\overline{V}_S(t) \geq 0$ represents the supply on the market for particular product $i = 1,...,n$. I denote $\overline{V}_D(t) \geq 0$ a non-negative vector of the products' demand on the market, where each non-negative component $[V_D(t)]_i \geq 0$ of the vector $\overline{V}_D(t) \geq 0$ represents the demand on the market for particular product $i = 1,...,n$. I denote $\overline{P}_R(t) \geq 0$ a non-negative vector of the products' prices on the market, where each non-negative component $[P_R(t)]_i \geq 0$ of the vector $\overline{P}_R(t) \geq 0$ represents the price on the market for particular product $i = 1,...,n$.

Now I introduce vector of the volumes of products' surpluses (or shortages) on the market

$$\hat{V}(t) = \left[(I - A)\overline{V}_S(t) - \overline{V}_D(t)\right] \tag{2.63}$$

where I is an identity matrix of size n.

As I mentioned in Chapter 1, for inverse matrix $(I - A)^{-1}$ to exist, and to be non-negative it is necessary and sufficient that Frobenius value of non-negative matrix A be less than one (see [2]).

Now I introduce into consideration the monetary market, and combine the monetary market described earlier by System (2.31 – 33) with the standalone products' market described in Chapter 1 by System (1.127 – 129).

At first I need to make an assumption how the changes in the rate of money's supply are affecting the demand for each individual product.

Proposition 5 Product Preferences in Multi-Product Economy

Changes in the rate of demand for each individual product on the market are linearly proportional to the changes in the rate of money's supply where proportions are fixed, and together are summed to one (income elasticity of the product's demand).

Mathematically it means the following,

$$\left[\frac{d^2V_D(t)}{dt^2}\right]_i = [\Psi]_i \frac{d^2M_S(t)}{dt^2} \tag{2.64}$$

where all $[\Psi]_i \geq 0$ elements of vector $\overline{\Psi} \geq 0$ are of constant value and $\sum_{i=1}^{n} [\Psi]_i = 1$.

On the other hand, the total demand for all products are equal to the money's supply through integrating condition connecting both the money's and the products' markets

$$M_S(t) = \sum_{i=1}^{n} [V_D(t)]_i \tag{2.65}$$

Therefore, the following integrated system of ordinary differential equations describes the economic forces of the joined markets for the products and money,

$$\frac{d\overline{P}_R(t)}{dt} = -\Lambda_P \left[(I - A)\overline{V}_S(t) - \overline{V}_D(t) \right] \tag{2.66}$$

$$\frac{dP_M(t)}{dt} = -\mu_P \left(M_S(t) - M_D(t) \right) \tag{2.67}$$

$$\frac{d^2\overline{V}_S(t)}{dt^2} = \Lambda_S \frac{d\overline{P}_R(t)}{dt} \tag{2.68}$$

$$\frac{d^2\overline{V}_D(t)}{dt^2} = -\Lambda_D \frac{d^2\overline{P}_R(t)}{dt^2} + \overline{\Psi}\, \mu_S \frac{dP_M(t)}{dt} \tag{2.69}$$

$$\frac{d^2 M_S(t)}{dt^2} = \mu_S \frac{dP_M(t)}{dt} - \sum_{i=1}^{n} [\Lambda_D]_{ii} \left[\frac{d^2 P_R(t)}{dt^2} \right]_i \tag{2.70}$$

$$\frac{d^2 M_D(t)}{dt^2} = -\mu_D \frac{d^2 P_M(t)}{dt^2} \tag{2.71}$$

where $t \geq t_0$ and Λ_S, Λ_D, Λ_P, –.diagonal matrices with non-negative constant elements on the main diagonals.

I introduce variable of the volumes of money' surpluses (or shortages) on the monetary market,

$$\hat{M}(t) = \sum_{i=1}^{n} [V_D(t)]_i - M_D(t) \tag{2.72}$$

and rewrite System (2.66 – 71) into the next one using introduced earlier vector $\hat{V}(t)$ and variable $\hat{M}(t)$,

$$\frac{d^2\hat{V}(t)}{dt^2} + \Lambda_P \Lambda_D \frac{d\hat{V}(t)}{dt} + \Lambda_P \Lambda_S (I - A)\hat{V}(t) = \mu_P\, \mu_S\, \overline{\Psi}\, \hat{M}(t) \tag{2.73}$$

$$\frac{d^2\hat{M}(t)}{dt^2} + \mu_P\,\mu_D\,\frac{d\hat{M}(t)}{dt} + \mu_P\,\mu_S\,\hat{M}(t) = \sum_{i=1}^{n}[\Lambda_P]_{ii}\,[\Lambda_D]_{ii}\left[\frac{d\hat{V}(t)}{dt}\right]_i \tag{2.74}$$

The routine way to solve such System (2.73 – 74), which contains nonhomogeneous linear second-order differential equations, is at first to represent it as the system of nonhomogeneous linear first-order differential equations, and secondly to use the property of such system (for example, see [18]) saying that general solution of a nonhomogeneous linear system of ordinary differential equations can be represented as sum of a particular solution of the nonhomogeneous linear system of ordinary differential equations and the general solution of the corresponding homogeneous linear system of ordinary differential equations.

Finally I note that I used a linear relationship between changes in the rate of money's supply and changes in the rate of demand for each individual product. Though it can be true for small changes in time and small changes of input (i.e. if to consider a snapshot of economy in time), it is definitely not true for big changes of inputs or time. For such situations one has to consider changes in the preferences with regard to the demand for each individual product on the market. I don't touch the subject where aforementioned changes in the preferences are directed in this book.

2.4 Stock Market

2.4.1 Outline of Markets' Hierarchy

Now I want to categorize relationships existing among different markets.

If one is studying the development of some particular market over long period of time I say that she is studying an economic growth (in a broad sense, i.e. both economic growth and decline). I describe the nature of economic growth in next Chapter.

If one is studying the development flourishing between two or more geographically distinct markets of the same products I say that she is studying an economic trade. I describe the nature of economic trade in next Chapter as well.

There are also situations when the products traded on one market are derivatives from the products traded on another market. One example is the stock market where one trades shares of different companies, which values in turn depend on the performance experienced by the products supplied by these companies on the market of products. Another example is the options market where one trades options (and other financial instruments) on equities, which values depend on the performance experienced by the companies' stock on the stock market. I say that in such situation one market is primary market and another one is derivative market (in the first example, market of products is primary market, and stock market is derivative market).

I describe in this section relationships that exist between primary and derivative markets.

2.4.2 Primary Market – Market for Products

The market for products (goods and services) was described in details in Chapter 1. Here I briefly repeat explanation of economic forces acting on such market. For simplicity I restrict myself to the market with one product.

When there are no disturbing economic forces, the market is in equilibrium position, i.e. the product's supply and demand are equal, and they are developing with a constant rate and the product's price is fixed.

When the balance between the product's supply and demand is broken, the product's market is experienced the economic forces, which act to bring the market to a new equilibrium position.

These economic forces are described by the following ordinary differential equations regarding to the product's supply $V_S(t)$, demand $V_D(t)$, and price $P_R(t)$,

$$\frac{dP_R(t)}{dt} = -\lambda_P \left(V_S(t) - V_D(t) \right) \tag{2.75}$$

$$\frac{d^2 V_S(t)}{dt^2} = \lambda_S \frac{dP_R(t)}{dt} \tag{2.76}$$

$$\frac{d^2 V_D(t)}{dt^2} = -\lambda_D \frac{d^2 P_R(t)}{dt^2} \tag{2.77}$$

In the equations above the values $\lambda_P, \lambda_S, \lambda_D \geq 0$ are constants.

The meaning of Equations (2.75 – 77) was described is as follows.

Let me define the product's shortage at each point in time as the negative difference between the product's supply and the one's demand. Similarly the product's surplus at the same time stands for the positive difference between the product's supply and demand. In situation when the product's demand and supply are equal, the market for product is at the equilibrium position.

When the product's demand and supply are not equal, the price of product changes. If the product's supply exceeds the one's demand, the price goes down, and it goes up in another circumstances. The rate of changes in the product's price at each point in time is developing with a pace inversely-linearly proportional to the product's shortage (or surplus) at the same time.

When the product's price changes, the product's supply undergoes changes as well. When the price increases, the product's supply goes up, and it goes down in another circumstances. The acceleration (or deceleration) of changes in the product's supply at each point in time is linearly proportional to the rate of changes in the product's price at the same time.

Also when the product's price changes, the product's demand experiences an oppressive effect. When the price increases, the product's demand goes down, and it goes up in another circumstances. The acceleration (or deceleration) of changes in the product's demand at each point in time is inversely-linearly proportional to the acceleration (or deceleration) of changes in the product's price at the same time.

2.4.3 Primary Market – Money Market

The market for peculiar product – money – was minutely described in section 2.3 of this Chapter. Here I briefly repeat some results of that section.

When there are no disturbing economic forces, the market is in equilibrium position, i.e. the money's supply and demand are equal, and they are developing with a constant rate and the money's price – represented by an interest rate – is fixed. I will talk more about interest rate in next Chapter.

When such balance between the money's supply and demand is broken, the money's market is experienced the economic forces, which act to bring the market to a new equilibrium position.

These market forces are described by the following ordinary differential equations regarding to the money's supply $M_S(t)$, demand $M_D(t)$, and price $P_M(t)$.

$$\frac{dP_M(t)}{dt} = -\mu_P (M_S(t) - M_D(t)) \tag{2.78}$$

$$\frac{d^2 M_S(t)}{dt^2} = \mu_S \frac{dP_M(t)}{dt} \tag{2.79}$$

$$\frac{d^2 M_D(t)}{dt^2} = -\mu_D \frac{d^2 P_M(t)}{dt^2} \tag{2.80}$$

In Equations (2.78 – 80) the values $\mu_P, \mu_S, \mu_D \geq 0$ are constants.

The meaning of equations above is as follows.

Let me define the positive difference between the money's supply and the one's demand at each point in time as the money's surplus. Likewise the money's shortage at the same time denotes the negative difference between the money's supply and demand. As earlier when money's demand and supply are equal, the money's market lies at the equilibrium position.

In situation when money's supply and demand are not equal, the price of money experiences changes. The price of money is expressed through an interest rate. If the money's supply exceeds the one's demand on the market, the price of money goes down, and it goes up in another circumstances. The rate of changes in the money's price at each point in time is developing with a pace inversely-linearly proportional to the money's shortage (or surplus) at the same time.

When the money's price changes, the money's supply undergoes changes. Likewise when the money's price increases, the money's supply goes up, and it goes down in another circumstances. The acceleration (or deceleration) of changes in the money's supply at each point in time is linearly proportional to the rate of changes in the money's price at the same time.

When the money's price changes, the money's demand experiences an oppressive effect as well. When the money's price increases, the money's demand goes down, and it goes up in another circumstances. The acceleration (or deceleration) of changes in the money's demand at each point in time is inversely-linearly proportional to the acceleration (or deceleration) of changes in the money's price at the same time.

2.4.4 Primary Market – Joined Market of Money and Products

I described dynamics of joined markets, which contain both single or multiple products and money, in section 2.3 of this Chapter. Here I go over results of that section describing the market with one product.

When there are no disturbing economic forces, both markets are in equilibrium positions. The product's supply and demand are equal, and they are developing with a constant rate and the product's price is fixed. The money's supply and demand on the monetary market are equal, and they are also developing with a constant rate and the money's price is fixed. The aforesaid rate, which relates to the product, equals to similar rate, which relates to money.

When the balance either between the product's supply and demand or between the money's supply and demand is broken the joined markets are experienced the economic forces, which act to bring them to new equilibrium positions.

These market forces are described by the following ordinary differential equations regarding to the product's supply $V_S(t)$, demand $V_D(t)$, and price $P_R(t)$ and the money's supply $M_S(t)$, demand $M_D(t)$, and price $P_M(t)$,

$$\frac{dP_R(t)}{dt} = -\lambda_P \left(V_S(t) - V_D(t)\right) \tag{2.81}$$

$$\frac{dP_M(t)}{dt} = -\mu_P \left(M_S(t) - M_D(t)\right) \tag{2.82}$$

$$\frac{d^2 V_S(t)}{dt^2} = \lambda_S \frac{dP_R(t)}{dt} \tag{2.83}$$

$$\frac{d^2 M_S(t)}{dt^2} = \mu_S \frac{dP_M(t)}{dt} - \lambda_D \frac{d^2 P_R(t)}{dt^2} \tag{2.84}$$

$$\frac{d^2 M_D(t)}{dt^2} = -\mu_D \frac{d^2 P_M(t)}{dt^2} \tag{2.85}$$

$$V_D(t) = M_S(t) \tag{2.86}$$

Meaning of Equations (2.81 – 86) is as follows.

As formerly I denote the product's shortage at each point in time as a negative difference between the product's supply and the one's demand. Similarly the product's surplus at the same time stands for a positive difference between the product's supply and demand. Likewise the negative difference between the money's supply and the one's demand at each point in time is the money's shortage. Equally the money's surplus at the same time denotes the positive difference between the money's supply and demand.

Also I identify the money's supply with the product's demand. It follows from the fact that the product's demand has to be solvent.

In situation when the product's supply and demand are equal, the market for product is in the equilibrium position. As well when the money's supply and demand are equal, the money's market lies in the equilibrium position.

When the product's demand (i.e. money's supply) and the product's supply are not equal, the price of product changes. If the product's supply exceeds the one's demand, the price goes down, and it goes up in another circumstances. The rate of changes in the product's price at each point in time is developing with a pace inversely-linearly proportional to the product's shortage (or surplus) at the same time.

When the product's price changes, the product's supply undergoes changes. When the price increases, the product's supply goes up, and it goes down in another circumstances. The acceleration (or deceleration) of changes in the product's supply at each point in time is linearly proportional to the rate of changes in the product's price at the same time.

Also when the product's price changes, the product's demand (i.e. money's supply) experiences an oppressive effect. When the price increases, the product's demand goes down, and it goes up in another circumstances. The acceleration (or deceleration) of changes in the product's demand at each point in time is inversely-linearly proportional to the acceleration (or deceleration) of changes in the product's price at the same time.

But distinct from the product's supply, the product's demand (i.e. money's supply) experiences an impact from the money's market.

In situation when the money's demand and the money's supply (i.e. product's demand) are not equal, the price of money experiences changes. As it was mentioned before the price of money is expressed through an interest rate. If the money's supply (i.e. product's demand) exceeds the one's demand on the monetary market, the price of money goes down, and it goes up in another circumstances. The rate of changes in the money's price at each point in time is developing with a pace inversely-linearly proportional to the money's shortage (or surplus) at the same time.

When the money's price changes, the money's supply (i.e. product's demand) undergoes changes. Correspondingly when the money's price increases, the money's supply (i.e. product's demand) goes up, and it goes down in another circumstances. The acceleration (or deceleration) of changes in the money's supply (i.e. product's demand) at each point in time is linearly proportional to the rate of changes in the money's price at the same time.

Also when the money's price changes, the money's demand experiences an oppressive effect. When the money's price increases, the money's demand goes down, and it goes up in another circumstances. The acceleration (or deceleration) of changes in the money's demand at each point in time is inversely-linearly proportional to the acceleration (or deceleration) of the changes in the money's price at the same time.

Thus there are two impacts on the money's supply (or product's demand). At first it is the effect from the product's price changes. Secondly, it is the effect from the money's price changes.

Here I give an illustrative example showing activities of economic forces in the joined markets.

Let me take in this example for simplicity that $\lambda_D = 0$ and $\mu_D = 0$.

I assume that at time $t = t_0$ the money's demand on the joined markets has changed. That situation was considered in section 2.3 for the following initial conditions on the monetary market $M_D(t_0) = \Delta \neq 0$, $M_S(t_0) = 0$, $\frac{dM_S(t_0)}{dt} = \frac{dM_D(t_0)}{dt} = 0$, $P_M(t_0) = P_M^0$, and on the market of product $V_S(t_0) = V_D(t_0) = 0$, $\frac{dV_S(t_0)}{dt} = \frac{dV_D(t_0)}{dt} = 0$, $P_R(t_0) = P_R^0$.

It was shown in section 2.3 (see Equation 2.42) that aforesaid change in the money's demand $M_D(t_0) = \Delta$ creates the following fluctuations in the product's supply $V_S(t)$,

$$V_S(t) = \Delta \left[\frac{\mu_P \mu_S}{\lambda_P \lambda_S - \mu_P \mu_S} \cos\left(\sqrt{\lambda_P \lambda_S}(t - t_0)\right) - \frac{\lambda_P \lambda_S}{\lambda_P \lambda_S - \mu_P \mu_S} \cos\left(\sqrt{\mu_P \mu_S}(t - t_0)\right) + 1 \right] \tag{2.87}$$

Solution (2.87) of this illustrative example represents the sum of two sinusoids.

2.4.5 Secondary Market – Market of Equities

Here I describe the market of equities. One trades there the shares of companies, and the values of these companies depend on two factors. The first factor is the performance of the products supplied by these companies on the market of products. The second factor is relation between demand and supply of companies' shares on the market of equities.

Now I formalize the impact of these factors and describe how the values of companies' shares are determined.

Economic forces performing the valuation of companies' shares relate the demand, supply, and prices of shares to the demand, supply, and prices of underlying products.

I restrict myself in this section to the theoretical model where primary market consists of two distinct products – the real product and money, and the secondary market (i.e. market of equities) assesses the value of company, which produces the real product. Thus the equity itself represents ownership rights on an entity producing the product in question and as a result ownership rights on the product in question as well.

Let me denote $V_S^{II}(t)$ – be supply of shares on the market of equities (the secondary market), $V_D^{II}(t)$ – be demand for shares on the market of equities, and $P_E(t)$ – be price of one share on the market of equities. Similarly I denote $M_S^{II}(t)$ – be supply of money on the market of equities, $M_D^{II}(t)$ – be demand for money on the market of equities, and $P_M^{II}(t)$ – be price of money on the market of equities.

Here I make an assumption about demand on the secondary market.

Hypothesis 7 Behavior of Demand Forces on Secondary Market

Demand for equities on the secondary market represents the sum of demand force for equities on the secondary market, and force proportional to supply force for product on the primary market.

Using expressions for demand and supply forces, the statement above mathematically means the following,

$$\frac{d^2V_D^{II}(t)}{dt^2} = -\lambda_D^{II}\frac{d^2P_R^{II}(t)}{dt^2} + \lambda_I^{II}\frac{dP_R(t)}{dt} \tag{2.88}$$

where $\lambda_D^{II} > 0$ and $\lambda_I^{II} > 0$.

Then I can write the following ordinary differential equations describing the economic forces on the market of equities,

$$\frac{dP_R(t)}{dt} = -\lambda_P\left(V_S(t) - V_D(t)\right) \tag{2.89}$$

$$\frac{dP_R^{II}(t)}{dt} = -\lambda_P^{II}\left(V_S^{II}(t) - V_D^{II}(t)\right) \tag{2.90}$$

$$\frac{d^2V_S^{II}(t)}{dt^2} = \lambda_S^{II}\frac{dP_R^{II}(t)}{dt} \tag{2.91}$$

$$\frac{d^2V_D^{II}(t)}{dt^2} = -\lambda_D^{II}\frac{d^2P_R^{II}(t)}{dt^2} + \lambda_I^{II}\frac{dP_R(t)}{dt} \tag{2.92}$$

In Equations (2.89 – 92) above the values $\lambda_I^{II}, \lambda_P^{II}, \lambda_S^{II}, \lambda_D^{II} \geq 0$ are constants.

The meaning of Equations (2.89 – 92) is following.

The market of equities lies in the equilibrium position, when both the demand and supply are equal on the market of products (the primary market) and the demand and supply are equal on the market of equities (the secondary market).

When the product's demand and supply are not equal, the price of product experiences changes. If the product's supply exceeds the one's demand on the primary market, the price of product goes down, and it goes up in another circumstances. The rate of changes in the product's price at each point in time is developing with a pace inversely-linearly proportional to the product's shortage (or surplus) at the same time.

When the product's price changes, the demand for underlying equities undergoes changes on the secondary market. Correspondingly when the product's price increases, the demand for underlying equities goes up, and it goes down in another circumstances. The acceleration (or deceleration) of changes in the demand for underlying equities at each point in time is linearly proportional to the rate of changes in the product's price at the same time.

In situation when the demand and supply of equities are not equal, the price of equities experiences changes. If the supply of equities exceeds the demand for ones on the market of equities (the secondary market), the price of equities goes down, and it goes up in another circumstances. The rate of changes in the price of equities at each point in time is developing with a pace inversely-linearly proportional to the shortage (or surplus) of equities at the same time.

When the price of equities changes, the supply of equities undergoes changes. Likewise when the price of equities increases, the supply of equities goes up, and it goes down in another circumstances. The acceleration (or deceleration) of changes in the supply of equities at each point in time is linearly proportional to the rate of changes in the price of equities at the same time.

Also when the price of equities changes, the demand for equities experiences an oppressive effect. When the price of equities increases, the demand for equities goes down, and it goes up in another circumstances. The acceleration (or deceleration) of changes in the demand for equities at each point in time is inversely-linearly proportional to the acceleration (or deceleration) of changes in the price of equities at the same time.

Here I give an illustrative example showing activities of economic forces.

Let me take in this example for simplicity that $\lambda_D = 0$ and $\lambda_D^{II} = 0$.

I assume that at time $t = t_0$ I have the following conditions on the primary and secondary markets – on the market of product $V_D(t_0) = \Delta \neq 0$, $V_S(t_0) = 0$, $\frac{dV_D(t_0)}{dt} = \frac{dV_S(t_0)}{dt} = 0$, $P_R(t_0) = P_R^0$, and on the market of equities $V_D^{II}(t_0) = V_S^{II}(t_0) = 0$, $\frac{dV_D^{II}(t_0)}{dt} = \frac{dV_S^{II}(t_0)}{dt} = 0$, $P_E(t_0) = P_E^0$.

Based on [18], [19] the aforesaid change in the product's demand $V_D(t_0) = \Delta$ creates the fluctuating disbalance between the product's supply and demand,

$$V_S(t) - V_D(t) = -\Delta \cos\left(\sqrt{\lambda_P \lambda_S}\,(t - t_0)\right) \tag{2.93}$$

that produces the fluctuating disbalance between supply and demand for underlying equities,

$$V_S^{II}(t) - V_D^{II}(t) = \frac{\Delta \lambda_P \lambda_I^{II}}{\lambda_P \lambda_S - \lambda_P^{II} \lambda_S^{II}} \left[\cos\left(\sqrt{\lambda_P \lambda_S}\,(t - t_0)\right) - \cos\left(\sqrt{\lambda_P^{II} \lambda_S^{II}}\,(t - t_0)\right)\right] \tag{2.94}$$

Therefore the price of equities on the market of equities fluctuates as follows,

$$P_E(t) = P_E^0 - \frac{\Delta \lambda_P \lambda_P^{II} \lambda_I^{II}}{\lambda_P \lambda_S - \lambda_P^{II} \lambda_S^{II}} \left[\frac{1}{\sqrt{\lambda_P \lambda_S}} \sin\left(\sqrt{\lambda_P \lambda_S}(t - t_0)\right) + \frac{1}{\sqrt{\lambda_P^{II} \lambda_S^{II}}} \sin\left(\sqrt{\lambda_P^{II} \lambda_S^{II}}(t - t_0)\right) \right] \tag{2.95}$$

The solution of this illustrative example denoted by Equation (2.95) represents the sum of two sinusoids.

2.4.6 Secondary Market – Joined Markets of Money and Equities

Similar to System (2.81 – 86) and System (2.89 – 92) I can write the ordinary differential equations describing the economic forces on the joined markets of money and equities,

$$\frac{dP_R(t)}{dt} = -\lambda_P \left(V_S(t) - V_D(t)\right) \tag{2.96}$$

$$\frac{dP_R^{II}(t)}{dt} = -\lambda_P^{II} \left(V_S^{II}(t) - V_D^{II}(t)\right) \tag{2.97}$$

$$\frac{dP_M^{II}(t)}{dt} = -\mu_P^{II} \left(M_S^{II}(t) - M_D^{II}(t)\right) \tag{2.98}$$

$$\frac{d^2V_S^{II}(t)}{dt^2} = \lambda_S^{II} \frac{dP_R^{II}(t)}{dt} \tag{2.99}$$

$$\frac{d^2 M_S^{II}(t)}{dt^2} = \mu_S^{II} \frac{dP_M^{II}(t)}{dt} - \lambda_D^{II} \frac{d^2 P_R^{II}(t)}{dt^2} + \lambda_I^{II} \frac{dP_R(t)}{dt} \tag{2.100}$$

$$\frac{d^2 M_D^{II}(t)}{dt^2} = -\mu_D^{II} \frac{d^2 P_M^{II}(t)}{dt^2} \tag{2.101}$$

$$V_D^{II}(t) = M_S^{II}(t) \tag{2.102}$$

The meaning of Equations (2.96 – 102) is following.

The joined markets of money and equities lie in the equilibrium position, when there are balances between the demand and supply on the market of products (the primary market), between the demand and supply on the market of money and between the demand and supply on the market of equities (the secondary markets).

When the product's demand and supply are not equal, the price of product experiences changes. If the product's supply exceeds the one's demand on the primary market, the price of product goes down, and it goes up in another circumstances. The rate of changes in the product's price at each point in time is developing with a pace inversely-linearly proportional to the product's shortage (or surplus) at the same time.

Since the demand for equities has to be solvent, I equate the money's supply on the secondary market with the demand for equities on the secondary market.

When the product's price changes, the demand for equities on the secondary market (or the money supply on the secondary market) undergoes changes as well. Correspondingly when the product's price increases, the demand for equities goes up, and it goes down in another circumstances. The acceleration (or deceleration) of changes in the demand for equities at each point in time is linearly proportional to the rate of changes in the product's price at the same time.

When the demand for equities (i.e. money's supply) and the supply of equities are not equal on the market of equities, the price of equities changes. If the supply of equities exceeds the demand for ones on the market of equities (the secondary market), the price of equities goes down, and it goes up in another circumstances. The rate of changes in the price of equities at each point in time is developing with a pace inversely-linearly proportional to the shortage (or surplus) of equities at the same time.

When the price of equities changes, the supply of equities undergoes changes. Likewise when the price of equities increases, the supply of equities goes up, and it goes down in another circumstances. The acceleration (or deceleration) of changes in the supply of equities at each point in time is linearly proportional to the rate of changes in the price of equities at the same time.

Also when the price of equities changes, the demand for equities (i.e. money's supply) experiences an oppressive effect. When the price of equities increases, the demand for equities goes down, and it goes up in another circumstances. The acceleration (or deceleration) of changes in the demand for equities at each point in time is inversely-linearly proportional to the acceleration (or deceleration) of changes in the price of equities at the same time.

But distinct from the supply of equities, the demand for equities (i.e. money's supply) on the market of equities experiences an impact from the money's market.

In situation when the money's demand and the money's supply (i.e. demand for equities) are not equal, the price of money experiences changes. As it was mentioned before the price of money is expressed through an interest rate. If the money's supply (i.e. demand for equities) exceeds the one's demand on the monetary market, the price of money goes down, and it goes up in another circumstances. The rate of changes in the money's price at each point in time is developing with a pace inversely-linearly proportional to the money's shortage (or surplus) at the same time.

When the price of money changes, the money's supply (i.e. demand for equities) experiences changes. Correspondingly when the money's price increases, the money's supply (i.e. demand for equities) goes up, and it goes down in another circumstances. The acceleration (or deceleration) of changes in the money's supply (i.e. demand for equities) at each point in time is linearly proportional to the rate of changes in the money's price at the same time.

Also when the money's price changes, the money's demand experiences an oppressive effect. When the money's price increases, the money's demand goes down, and it goes up in another circumstances. The acceleration (or deceleration) of changes in the money's demand at each point in time is inversely-linearly proportional to the acceleration (or deceleration) of the changes in the money's price at the same time.

Thus there are three impacts on the demand for equities (or the money's supply) on the market of equities. At first it is the effect from the product's price changes on the market of products. Secondly, it is the effect from changes in the price of equities. Thirdly, it is the effect from changes in the price of money.

I have to admit that at each point in time the price of money supplied for the purchase of equities on the secondary market has to be equal to the price of money supplied for the purchase of product on the primary market. Otherwise it can create so-called *arbitrage opportunity* for one who trades on both primary and secondary markets. However I postpone discussion of arbitrage until next Chapter.

2.4.7 Tertiary Market – Market of Derivatives

Here I describe the market of derivatives. One trades there the rights to obtain (dispose) the shares of companies, and the values of these rights depend on three factors. The first factor is the performance of the products supplied by these companies on the market of products. The second factor is the performance of the companies' shares on the market of equities. The third factor is relation between demand and supply of the rights on companies' shares on the market of derivatives.

Now I formalize the impact of these factors and describe how the values of rights on companies' shares are determined.

Economic forces performing the valuation of rights to obtain (dispose) the companies' shares relate the demand, supply, and prices of rights on the shares to the demand, supply, and prices of the shares themselves and underlying products supplied by the companies.

I restrict myself in this section to the theoretical model where primary market consists of two distinct products – the real product and money, the secondary market (i.e. market of equities) assesses the value of company, which produces the real product, and the tertiary market (i.e. market of derivatives) assesses the value of rights to obtain (dispose) the company's shares. Thus the derivative represents ownership rights to obtain (dispose) rights on an entity producing the product in question, and as consequence ownership rights to obtain (dispose) rights on the product in question as well.

Let me denote $V_S^{III}(t)$ – be supply of derivatives on the market of derivatives (the tertiary market), $V_D^{III}(t)$ – be demand for derivatives on the market of derivatives, and $P_D(t)$ – be price of derivatives on the market of derivatives. Similarly I denote $M_S^{III}(t)$ – be supply of money on the market of derivatives, $M_D^{III}(t)$ – be demand for money on the market of derivatives, and $P_M^{III}(t)$ – be price of money on the market of derivatives.

Here I make an assumption about demand on the tertiary market.

Hypothesis 8 Behavior of Demand Forces on Tertiary Market

Demand for derivatives on the tertiary market represents the sum of demand force for derivatives on the tertiary market, force proportional to supply force for equities on the secondary market, and force proportional to supply force for product on the primary market.

Using expressions for demand and supply forces, the statement above mathematically means the following,

$$\frac{d^2V_D^{III}(t)}{dt^2} = -\lambda_D^{III}\frac{d^2P_R^{III}(t)}{dt^2} + \lambda_{II}^{III}\frac{dP_R^{II}(t)}{dt} + \lambda_I^{III}\frac{dP_R(t)}{dt} \tag{2.103}$$

where $\lambda_D^{III} > 0$, $\lambda_{II}^{III} > 0$ and $\lambda_I^{III} > 0$.

Then I can write the following ordinary differential equations describing the economic forces on the market of derivatives,

$$\frac{dP_R(t)}{dt} = -\lambda_P\left(V_S(t) - V_D(t)\right) \tag{2.104}$$

$$\frac{dP_R^{II}(t)}{dt} = -\lambda_P^{II}\left(V_S^{II}(t) - V_D^{II}(t)\right) \tag{2.105}$$

$$\frac{dP_R^{III}(t)}{dt} = -\lambda_P^{III}\left(V_S^{III}(t) - V_D^{III}(t)\right) \tag{2.106}$$

$$\frac{d^2V_S^{III}(t)}{dt^2} = \lambda_S^{III}\frac{dP_R^{III}(t)}{dt} \tag{2.107}$$

$$\frac{d^2V_D^{III}(t)}{dt^2} = -\lambda_D^{III}\frac{d^2P_R^{III}(t)}{dt^2} + \lambda_{II}^{III}\frac{dP_R^{II}(t)}{dt} + \lambda_I^{III}\frac{dP_R(t)}{dt} \tag{2.108}$$

In Equations (2.104 – 108) above the values $\lambda_I^{III}, \lambda_{II}^{III}, \lambda_P^{III}, \lambda_S^{III}, \lambda_D^{III} \geq 0$ are constants.

The meaning of Equations (2.104 – 108) is following.

The market of derivatives lies in the equilibrium position, when simultaneously the demand and supply are equal on the market of products (the primary market), the demand and supply are equal on the market of equities (the secondary market), and the demand and supply are equal on the market of derivatives (the tertiary market).

When the product's demand and supply are not equal, the price of product experiences changes. If the product's supply exceeds the one's demand on the primary market, the price of product goes down, and it goes up in another circumstances. The rate of changes in the product's price at each point in time is developing with a pace inversely-linearly proportional to the product's shortage (or surplus) at the same time.

Similarly when the demand and supply of equities are not equal, the price of equities experiences changes. If the supply of equities exceeds the demand for ones on the secondary market, the price of equities goes down, and it goes up in another circumstances. The rate of changes in the price of equities at each point in time is developing with a pace inversely-linearly proportional to the shortage (or surplus) of equities at the same time.

When the price of product or the price of equities changes, the demand for underlying derivatives undergoes changes. Correspondingly when the price of product or the price of equities increases, the demand for underlying derivatives goes up, and it goes down in another circumstances. The acceleration (or deceleration) of changes in the demand for underlying derivatives at each point in time is linearly proportional to the rate of changes in the price of product or the price of equities at the same time.

When the demand and supply of derivatives are not equal, the price of derivatives experiences changes. If the supply of derivatives exceeds the demand for ones on the market of derivatives, the price of derivatives goes down, and it goes up in another circumstances. The rate of changes in the price of derivatives at each point in time is developing with a pace inversely-linearly proportional to the shortage (or surplus) of derivatives at the same time.

When the price of derivatives changes, the supply of derivatives undergoes changes. Correspondingly when the price of derivatives increases, the supply of derivatives goes up, and it goes down in another circumstances. The acceleration (or deceleration) of changes in the supply of derivatives at each point in time is linearly proportional to the rate of changes in the price of derivatives at the same time.

Also when the price of derivatives changes, the demand for derivatives experiences an oppressive effect. When the price of derivatives increases, the demand for derivatives goes down, and it goes up in another circumstances. The acceleration (or deceleration) of changes in the demand for derivatives at each point in time is inversely-linearly proportional to the acceleration (or deceleration) of changes in the price of derivatives at the same time.

Thus there are three impacts on the demand for derivatives on the tertiary market. At first it is the effect from the product's price changes on the market of products. Secondly, it is the effect from changes in the price of equities on the secondary market. Thirdly, it is the effect from the changes in the prices of derivatives themselves.

Here to avoid *the arbitrage opportunity* it is required that values of rights to obtain (dispose) the company's shares do not exceed the values of company's shares themselves. As I mentioned above the discussion of arbitrage will be presented in Chapter 3.

2.4.8 Tertiary Market – Joined Markets of Money and Derivatives

Again I can write the ordinary differential equations describing the economic forces on the joined markets of money and derivative,

$$\frac{dP_R(t)}{dt} = -\lambda_P \left(V_S(t) - V_D(t)\right) \tag{2.109}$$

$$\frac{dP_R^{II}(t)}{dt} = -\lambda_P^{II} \left(V_S^{II}(t) - V_D^{II}(t)\right) \tag{2.110}$$

$$\frac{dP_R^{III}(t)}{dt} = -\lambda_P^{III} \left(V_S^{III}(t) - V_D^{III}(t)\right) \tag{2.111}$$

$$\frac{dP_M^{III}(t)}{dt} = -\mu_P^{III}\left(M_S^{III}(t) - M_D^{III}(t)\right) \tag{2.112}$$

$$\frac{d^2V_S^{III}(t)}{dt^2} = \lambda_S^{III}\frac{dP_R^{III}(t)}{dt} \tag{2.113}$$

$$\frac{d^2M_S^{III}(t)}{dt^2} = \mu_S^{III}\frac{dP_M^{III}(t)}{dt} - \lambda_D^{III}\frac{d^2P_R^{III}(t)}{dt^2} + \lambda_{II}^{III}\frac{dP_R^{II}(t)}{dt} + \lambda_I^{III}\frac{dP_R(t)}{dt} \tag{2.114}$$

$$\frac{d^2M_D^{III}(t)}{dt^2} = -\mu_D^{III}\frac{d^2P_M^{III}(t)}{dt^2} \tag{2.115}$$

$$V_D^{III}(t) = M_S^{III}(t) \tag{2.116}$$

The meaning of Equations (2.109 – 116) is following.

The joined markets of money and derivatives lie in the equilibrium position, when there are balances between the demand and supply on the market of products (the primary market), between the demand and supply on the market of equities (the secondary market), and between the demand and supply on the market of money and between the demand and supply on the market of derivatives (the tertiary markets).

When the product's demand and supply are not equal, the price of product experiences changes. If the product's supply exceeds the one's demand on the primary market, the price of product goes down, and it goes up in another circumstances. The rate of changes in the product's price at each point in time is developing with a pace inversely-linearly proportional to the product's shortage (or surplus) at the same time.

Similarly when the demand and supply of equities are not equal, the price of equities experiences changes. If the supply of equities exceeds the demand for ones on the secondary market, the price of equities goes down, and it goes up in another circumstances. The rate of changes in the price of equities at each point in time is developing with a pace inversely-linearly proportional to the shortage (or surplus) of equities at the same time.

Since the demand for derivatives has to be solvent, I equate the money's supply on the tertiary market with the demand for derivatives on the tertiary market.

When the price of product or the price of equities changes, the demand for underlying derivatives undergoes changes. Correspondingly when the price of product or the price of equities increases, the demand for underlying derivatives goes up, and it goes down in another circumstances. The acceleration (or deceleration) of changes in the demand for underlying derivatives at each point in time is linearly proportional to the rate of changes in the price of product or the price of equities at the same time.

When the demand for derivatives (i.e. money's supply) and the supply of derivatives are not equal on the market of derivatives, the price of derivatives changes. If the supply of derivatives exceeds the demand for ones on the market of derivatives (the tertiary market), the price of derivatives goes down, and it goes up in another circumstances. The rate of changes in the price of derivatives at each point in time is developing with a pace inversely-linearly proportional to the shortage (or surplus) of derivatives at the same time.

When the price of derivatives changes, the supply of derivatives undergoes changes. Likewise when the price of derivatives increases, the supply of derivatives goes up, and it goes down in another circumstances. The acceleration (or deceleration) of changes in the supply of derivatives at each point in time is linearly proportional to the rate of changes in the price of derivatives at the same time.

Also when the price of derivatives changes, the demand for derivatives (i.e. money's supply) experiences an oppressive effect. When the price of derivatives increases, the demand for derivatives goes down, and it goes up in another circumstances. The acceleration (or deceleration) of changes in the demand for derivatives at each point in time is inversely-linearly proportional to the acceleration (or deceleration) of changes in the price of derivatives at the same time.

But distinct from the supply of equities, the demand for derivatives (i.e. money's supply) on the market of derivatives experiences an impact from the money's market.

In situation when the money's demand and the money's supply (i.e. demand for derivatives) are not equal, the price of money experiences changes. As it was mentioned earlier the price of money is expressed through an interest rate. If the money's supply (i.e. demand for derivatives) exceeds the one's demand on the monetary market, the price of money goes down, and it goes up in another circumstances. The rate of changes in the money's price at each point in time is developing with a pace inversely-linearly proportional to the money's shortage (or surplus) at the same time.

When the price of money changes, the money's supply (i.e. demand for derivatives) experiences changes. Correspondingly when the money's price increases, the money's supply (i.e. demand for derivatives) goes up, and it goes down in another circumstances. The acceleration (or deceleration) of changes in the money's supply (i.e. demand for derivatives) at each point in time is linearly proportional to the rate of changes in the money's price at the same time.

Also when the money's price changes, the money's demand experiences an oppressive effect. When the money's price increases, the money's demand goes down, and it goes up in another circumstances. The acceleration (or deceleration) of changes in the money's demand at each point in time is inversely-linearly proportional to the acceleration (or deceleration) of the changes in the money's price at the same time.

Thus there are four impacts on the demand for derivatives (or the money's supply) on the market of equities. At first it is the effect from the product's price changes on the market of products. Secondly, it is the effect from changes in the price of equities on the market of equities. Thirdly, it is the effect from changes in the price of derivatives. Fourthly, it is the effect from changes in the price of money.

2.5 Summary

In the second Chapter I described the models, which were focusing on the monetary aspects of the economy. I described why the prices rise in economy and showed that the effect of the prices' growth can be either temporal or permanent. I presented the role of monetary market and demonstrated its connection with real markets in economy. Lastly I explained the markets' hierarchy and revealed relationship among the markets of products (as a primary market), the markets of equities (as a secondary market), and the markets of derivatives (as a tertiary market).

In next Chapter I describe the models, which are focusing on the inter-market dynamics inside economic systems. I investigate an economic growth as a temporal development of one market, and economic trade as a spatial relationship among two and more markets. I also look at the phenomenon of market arbitrage, which brings different markets to the one-common-level equilibrium point.

Chapter 3

ECONOMIC GROWTH, TRADE, AND ARBITRAGE

3.1 INTRODUCTION

In this chapter, I describe three topics.

The first one is the concept of economic growth. I show that economic growth is caused by products' and money's savings.

The second topic is the concept of economic trade. I present mathematical models describing the economic trade both on the market of products, and on the monetary market.

The third topic is the concept of market arbitrage. I define the market arbitrage as interactions between local and global markets and describe mathematical models explaining market arbitrage both for the market of products, and for the monetary market.

Most material of this Chapter is new and original.

3.2 ECONOMIC GROWTH

3.2.1 Savings on Market for Single Product

Here in this section I show how the process of savings affects the situation on the market of products. For simplicity I restrict myself to the market with one product.

When there are no disturbing economic forces, the market is in equilibrium position, i.e. the product's supply and demand are equal, and they are developing with a constant rate and the product's price is fixed.

When the balance between the product's supply and demand is broken, the product's market is experienced the economic forces, which act to bring the market to a new equilibrium position.

These economic forces are described by the following ordinary differential equations regarding to the product's supply $V_S(t)$, demand $V_D(t)$, and price $P_R(t)$,

$$\frac{dP_R(t)}{dt} = -\lambda_P \left(V_S(t) - V_D(t)\right) \tag{3.1}$$

$$\frac{d^2V_S(t)}{dt^2} = \lambda_S \frac{dP_R(t)}{dt} \tag{3.2}$$

$$\frac{d^2V_D(t)}{dt^2} = -\lambda_D \frac{d^2P_R(t)}{dt^2} \tag{3.3}$$

In Equations (3.1 – 3) above the values $\lambda_P, \lambda_S, \lambda_D \geq 0$ are constants.

I present example describing the situation of product's saving. I assume that the market had been in equilibrium position until time $t = t_0$, the volumes of product's supply $V_S(t)$ and demand $V_D(t)$ on the market were equal, and they both were developing with constant rate r_D^0.

$$V_D(t) = r_D^0 (t - t_0) + V_D^0 \tag{3.4}$$

$$V_S(t) = V_D(t) \tag{3.5}$$

where $V_D(t_0) = V_D^0$.

At some point in time $t = t_0$ the equilibrium situation was broken, and the amount of product equal to $\Delta_R > 0$ was removed from the market,

$$V_S(t) = \begin{cases} V_D(t), & t < t_0 \\ V_D^0 - \Delta_R, & t = t_0 \end{cases} \tag{3.6}$$

where $0 < \Delta_R \leq V_D^0$.

That scenario increases at time $t = t_0$ the amount of savings $S_R(t)$ for the product,

$$S_R(t) = \begin{cases} S_R^0, & t < t_0 \\ S_R^0 + \Delta_R, & t = t_0 \end{cases} \tag{3.7}$$

where $S_R(t) = S_R^0$ for $t < t_0$.

From Equations (3.1 – 3) the volume of product's surplus (or shortage) $[V_S(t) - V_D(t)]$ for $t > t_0$ is described by,

$$\frac{d^2}{dt^2}(V_S(t) - V_D(t)) + \lambda_P \lambda_D \frac{d}{dt}(V_S(t) - V_D(t)) + \lambda_P \lambda_S (V_S(t) - V_D(t)) = 0 \tag{3.8}$$

with the following initial conditions,

$$V_S(t_0) - V_D(t_0) = -\Delta_R,$$

$$\frac{d}{dt}\left(V_S(t_0) - V_D(t_0)\right) = 0.$$

Initial conditions for the product's price $P_R(t)$ are $P_R(t_0) = P_R^0$ and $\frac{dP_R(t_0)}{dt} = \lambda_P \Delta_R$.

Similar from Equations (3.1 – 3) the product's price $P_R(t)$ is described by the following second-order ordinary differential equation for $t > t_0$,

$$\frac{d^2 P_R(t)}{dt^2} + \lambda_P \lambda_D \frac{dP_R(t)}{dt} + \lambda_P \lambda_S P_R(t) + C = 0 \tag{3.9}$$

where $C = -\lambda_P\left(\lambda_P \lambda_D \Delta_R + \lambda_S P_R^0\right)$ is a constant.

If I use new variable $P_1(t) = P_R(t) - P_R^0 - \frac{\lambda_P \lambda_D}{\lambda_S}\Delta_R$, Equation (3.9) becomes,

$$\frac{d^2 P_1(t)}{dt^2} + \lambda_P \lambda_D \frac{dP_1(t)}{dt} + \lambda_P \lambda_S P_1(t) = 0 \tag{3.10}$$

Therefore the initial conditions for $P_1(t)$ are $P_1(t_0) = -\frac{\lambda_P \lambda_D}{\lambda_S}\Delta_R$ and $\frac{dP_1(t_0)}{dt} = \lambda_P \Delta_R$.

Equations (3.8) and (3.10) have the same characteristic equation. And the roots of this characteristic equation are,

$$k_{1,2} = -\frac{\lambda_P \lambda_D}{2} \pm \sqrt{\frac{\lambda_P^2 \lambda_D^2}{4} - \lambda_P \lambda_S} \tag{3.11}$$

(a) If $\frac{\lambda_P^2 \lambda_D^2}{4} > \lambda_P \lambda_S$ the solution of Equation (3.8) is,

$$V_S(t) - V_D(t) = C_1 \exp\{k_1 (t - t_0)\} + C_2 \exp\{k_2 (t - t_0)\}, \tag{3.12}$$

where $C_1 = \Delta_R \dfrac{k_2}{k_1 - k_2}$ and $C_2 = \Delta_R \dfrac{k_1}{k_2 - k_1}$.

At situation above the solution of Equation (3.10) is

$$P_1(t) = C_3 \exp\{k_1(t - t_0)\} + C_4 \exp\{k_2(t - t_0)\}, \tag{3.13}$$

where $C_3 = \lambda_P \Delta_R \dfrac{1 - (\lambda_D/\lambda_S)k_2}{k_1 - k_2}$ and $C_4 = \lambda_P \Delta_R \dfrac{1 - (\lambda_D/\lambda_S)k_1}{k_2 - k_1}$ are constants.

Since $k_1 < 0$ and $k_2 < 0$ it takes place $V_S(t) - V_D(t) \to 0$ and $P_1(t) \to 0$ for $t \to +\infty$.

Since it was defined,

$$P_R(t) = P_1(t) + P_R^0 + \frac{\lambda_P \lambda_D}{\lambda_S} \Delta_R \tag{3.14}$$

it takes place for $t \to +\infty$,

$$P_R(t) \to P_R^0 + \frac{\lambda_P \lambda_D}{\lambda_S} \Delta_R \tag{3.15}$$

Since $V_D(t_0) = V_D^0$ and $\dfrac{dV_D(t_0)}{dt} = r_D^0$ it takes place from Equation (3.3),

$$V_D(t) = -\lambda_D P_1(t) + (r_D^0 + \lambda_P \lambda_D \Delta_R)(t - t_0) + V_D^0 - \frac{\lambda_P \lambda_D^2}{\lambda_S} \Delta_R \tag{3.16}$$

Since $V_S(t) - V_D(t) \to 0$ it takes place $V_S(t) \to V_D(t)$ for $t \to +\infty$.

I calculate now the effect of the product's savings by comparing two values taken at the limit $t \to +\infty$ where market of product comes to equilibrium. The first value is the product $v_R = P_R(t) \times V_D(t)$ of the product's price $P_R(t)$ and the product's demand $V_D(t)$ after savings. The second value is the product $\tilde{v}_R = \tilde{P}_R(t) \times \tilde{V}_D(t)$ of the product's price $\tilde{P}_R(t) = P_R^0$ and the product's demand $\tilde{V}_D(t) = r_D^0(t - t_0) + V_D^0$ if there is no withdrawal of savings from market of products.

Since $\lim\limits_{t \to +\infty} \left(\dfrac{P_R(t)}{\tilde{P}_R(t)} \right) = 1 + \dfrac{\lambda_P \lambda_D \Delta_R}{\lambda_S P_R^0}$ and $\lim\limits_{t \to +\infty} \left(\dfrac{V_D(t)}{\tilde{V}_D(t)} \right) = 1 + \dfrac{\lambda_P \lambda_D \Delta_R}{r_D^0}$ it takes place,

$$\lim_{t\to+\infty}\left(\frac{v_R(t)}{\widetilde{v}_R(t)}\right)=\lim_{t\to+\infty}\left(\frac{P_R(t)\times V_D(t)}{\widetilde{P}_R(t)\times\widetilde{V}_D(t)}\right)=1+\frac{\lambda_P\,\lambda_D\,\Delta_R}{\lambda_S\,P_R^0\,r_D^0}\left(\lambda_S\,P_R^0+r_D^0+\lambda_P\,\lambda_D\,\Delta_R\right) \tag{3.17}$$

(b) If $\frac{\lambda_P^2\,\lambda_D^2}{4}=\lambda_P\,\lambda_S$ the solution of Equation (3.8) is,

$$V_S(t)-V_D(t)=\left(C_1+C_2\left(t-t_0\right)\right)\exp\left\{-\frac{\lambda_P\,\lambda_D}{2}\left(t-t_0\right)\right\}, \tag{3.18}$$

where $C_1=-\Delta_R$ and $C_2=-\frac{\lambda_P\,\lambda_D}{2}\Delta_R$.

At situation above the solution of Equation (3.10) is

$$P_1(t)=\left(C_3+C_4\left(t-t_0\right)\right)\exp\left\{-\frac{\lambda_P\,\lambda_D}{2}\left(t-t_0\right)\right\}, \tag{3.19}$$

where $C_3=-\frac{\lambda_P\,\lambda_D}{\lambda_S}\Delta_R$ and $C_4=-\lambda_P\,\Delta_R$ are constants.

Since $\lambda_P\,\lambda_D>0$ it takes place $V_S(t)-V_D(t)\to 0$ and $P_1(t)\to 0$ for $t\to+\infty$.

Therefore it takes place for $t\to+\infty$,

$$P_R(t)\to P_R^0+\frac{\lambda_P\,\lambda_D}{\lambda_S}\Delta_R \tag{3.20}$$

as before,

$$V_D(t)=-\lambda_D\,P_1(t)+\left(r_D^0+\lambda_P\,\lambda_D\,\Delta_R\right)\left(t-t_0\right)+V_D^0-\frac{\lambda_P\,\lambda_D^2}{\lambda_S}\Delta_R \tag{3.21}$$

and $V_S(t)\to V_D(t)$ for $t\to+\infty$.

Since $\lim_{t\to+\infty}\left(\frac{P_R(t)}{\widetilde{P}_R(t)}\right)=1+\frac{\lambda_P\,\lambda_D\,\Delta_R}{\lambda_S\,P_R^0}$ and $\lim_{t\to+\infty}\left(\frac{V_D(t)}{\widetilde{V}_D(t)}\right)=1+\frac{\lambda_P\,\lambda_D\,\Delta_R}{r_D^0}$ it takes place,

$$\lim_{t\to+\infty}\left(\frac{v_R(t)}{\widetilde{v}_R(t)}\right)=\lim_{t\to+\infty}\left(\frac{P_R(t)\times V_D(t)}{\widetilde{P}_R(t)\times\widetilde{V}_D(t)}\right)=1+\frac{\lambda_P\,\lambda_D\,\Delta_R}{\lambda_S\,P_R^0\,r_D^0}\left(\lambda_S\,P_R^0+r_D^0+\lambda_P\,\lambda_D\,\Delta_R\right) \tag{3.22}$$

(c) If $\frac{\lambda_P^2 \lambda_D^2}{4} < \lambda_P \lambda_S$ the solution of Equation (3.8) is,

$$V_S(t) - V_D(t) = \exp\left\{-\frac{\lambda_P \lambda_D}{2}(t - t_0)\right\}$$

$$\times\left(C_1 \cos\left(\sqrt{\lambda_P \lambda_S - \frac{\lambda_P^2 \lambda_D^2}{4}}(t - t_0)\right) + C_2 \sin\left(\sqrt{\lambda_P \lambda_S - \frac{\lambda_P^2 \lambda_D^2}{4}}(t - t_0)\right)\right) \tag{3.23}$$

where $C_1 = -\Delta_R$ and $C_2 = \frac{-\lambda_P \lambda_D \Delta_R}{2\sqrt{\lambda_P \lambda_S - \frac{\lambda_P^2 \lambda_D^2}{4}}}$.

At situation above the solution of Equation (3.10) is

$$P_1(t) = \exp\left\{-\frac{\lambda_P \lambda_D}{2}(t - t_0)\right\}$$

$$\times\left(C_3 \cos\left(\sqrt{\lambda_P \lambda_S - \frac{\lambda_P^2 \lambda_D^2}{4}}(t - t_0)\right) + C_4 \sin\left(\sqrt{\lambda_P \lambda_S - \frac{\lambda_P^2 \lambda_D^2}{4}}(t - t_0)\right)\right) \tag{3.24}$$

where $C_3 = -\frac{\lambda_P \lambda_D}{\lambda_S}\Delta_R$ and $C_4 = \frac{\lambda_P \Delta_R}{\sqrt{\lambda_P \lambda_S - \frac{\lambda_P^2 \lambda_D^2}{4}}}\left(1 - \frac{\lambda_P \lambda_D^2}{2\lambda_S}\right)$ are constants.

Since $\lambda_P \lambda_D > 0$ it takes place $V_S(t) - V_D(t) \to 0$ and $P_1(t) \to 0$ for $t \to +\infty$. Therefore it takes place for $t \to +\infty$,

$$P_R(t) \to P_R^0 + \frac{\lambda_P \lambda_D}{\lambda_S}\Delta_R \tag{3.25}$$

as before,

$$V_D(t) = -\lambda_D P_1(t) + \left(r_D^0 + \lambda_P \lambda_D \Delta_R\right)(t - t_0) + V_D^0 - \frac{\lambda_P \lambda_D^2}{\lambda_S}\Delta_R \tag{3.26}$$

and $V_S(t) \to V_D(t)$ for $t \to +\infty$.

Since $\lim_{t \to +\infty}\left(\frac{P_R(t)}{\widetilde{P}_R(t)}\right) = 1 + \frac{\lambda_P \lambda_D \Delta_R}{\lambda_S P_R^0}$ and $\lim_{t \to +\infty}\left(\frac{V_D(t)}{\widetilde{V}_D(t)}\right) = 1 + \frac{\lambda_P \lambda_D \Delta_R}{r_D^0}$ it takes place,

$$\lim_{t \to +\infty}\left(\frac{v_R(t)}{\widetilde{v}_R(t)}\right) = \lim_{t \to +\infty}\left(\frac{P_R(t) \times V_D(t)}{\widetilde{P}_R(t) \times \widetilde{V}_D(t)}\right) = 1 + \frac{\lambda_P \lambda_D \Delta_R}{\lambda_S P_R^0 r_D^0}\left(\lambda_S P_R^0 + r_D^0 + \lambda_P \lambda_D \Delta_R\right) \tag{3.27}$$

Thus I covered all cases.

Therefore in the limit for $t \to +\infty$ withdrawal of part of the product from market cause both an increase of the product's price and an increase of product's supply. These actions raise the value $v_R(t)$ of product on the market.

That concludes the section.

3.2.2 Products' Savings and Economic Growth

It is not the first time I describe the concept of economic growth.

In [3] I presented a discrete model where the economic growth on the market of single product was taken into consideration through multiplying the product's investment (or savings) amount by a linear multiplier $(1+\alpha)$ with $\alpha \geq 0$. However soon after I abandoned this approach since it didn't explain the internal nature of economic growth and treated latter one as a "black box".

In [7] I presented a continuous model where the economic growth on the market of single product was taken into consideration through expressing the rate of product's supply as being proportional to the product's investment (or savings) amount. This approach gave quite interesting results. However later I rejected it also since it created the growth of economic flows, which would disagree with the law of *conservation of energy* and produce *perpetual motion* in economy.

Thus in this book the concept of economic growth is presented through dual impacts of changes in the product's prices and changes in the product's demand.

At first I want to stress out when I am talking about product's demand or supply I mean the demand or supply in the monetary form and not in natural form. This is especially important when I describe the monetary market and assume that money supply is equal to the product's demand. Secondly, one can conclude from the mentioned above that the product's price is not an absolute value since monetary value multiplied by monetary price is an economical nonsense but rather a dimensionless quantity such as a relative price.

Now let me return back to the concept of economic growth. To improve the product's quality one has to make an appropriate investment of the same or different products. It is done by applying the process of product's savings that withdraws a proper amount of product from the market. By doing so, one creates a temporal or permanent shortage of product on the market, which drives the product's price up. Hence when one pays an increased price for an improved product, from an economic point of view she compensates for the product's price increase caused by withdrawal of suitable amount of product from the market through the process of savings (or investment) in order to improve the product's quality.

On the other hand, withdrawing products from the market to perform savings decreases available amounts of products there. The reduced amount of products on the market is offset through an increased products' supply. Thus withdrawing products from the market by investors and replenishing products on the market by suppliers have opposite effects on the market situation. As a result it could remain more or fewer products on the market but always at an increased price. These mutual impacts drive the value of remained products on the market in different directions – increased price drives the value up, if quantity increases it drives the value up, and if quantity decreases it drives the value down. When the value increases one is talking about economic growth, and when the value decreases she is talking about economic recession.

I want to note that investments made into economy and aimed to the local market, which were not matched by the corresponding savings (for example such as investments made by foreign investors), do not create a growth in local economy. The trick is that foreign investments do not drive up prices of locally produced products (and services) that would increase the wealth of local economy. However when foreign investments are done to improve qualities of products that are targeting overseas markets then it creates a growth in local economy.

3.2.3 Savings on Money Market

Here in this section I show how the process of savings affects the situation on the monetary market.

When there are no disturbing economic forces, the monetary market is in equilibrium position, i.e. the money's supply and demand are equal, and they are developing with a constant rate and the money's price is fixed.

When the balance between the money's supply and demand is broken, the monetary market is experienced the economic forces, which act to bring the market to a new equilibrium position.

These economic forces are described by the following ordinary differential equations regarding to the money's supply $M_S(t)$, demand $M_D(t)$, and price $P_M(t)$,

$$\frac{dP_M(t)}{dt} = -\mu_P \left(M_S(t) - M_D(t)\right) \tag{3.28}$$

$$\frac{d^2 M_S(t)}{dt^2} = \mu_S \frac{dP_M(t)}{dt} \tag{3.29}$$

$$\frac{d^2 M_D(t)}{dt^2} = -\mu_D \frac{d^2 P_M(t)}{dt^2} \tag{3.30}$$

In Equations (3.28 – 30) the values $\mu_P, \mu_S, \mu_D \geq 0$ are constants.

Again I consider an example describing the situation of money's saving. I assume that the market had been in equilibrium position until time $t = t_0$, the volumes of money's supply $M_S(t)$ and demand $M_D(t)$ on the market were equal, and they both were developing with constant rate m_D^0.

$$M_D(t) = m_D^0 (t - t_0) + M_D^0 \tag{3.31}$$

$$M_S(t) = M_D(t) \tag{3.32}$$

where $M_D(t_0) = M_D^0$.

At some point in time $t = t_0$ the equilibrium situation was broken, and the amount of money equal to $\Lambda_M > 0$ was removed from the market,

$$M_S(t) = \begin{cases} M_D(t), & t < t_0 \\ M_D^0 - \Delta_M, & t = t_0 \end{cases} \tag{3.33}$$

where $0 < \Delta_M \leq M_D^0$.

That scenario increases at time $t = t_0$ the amount of money's savings $S_M(t)$,

$$S_M(t) = \begin{cases} S_M^0, & t < t_0 \\ S_M^0 + \Delta_M, & t = t_0 \end{cases} \tag{3.34}$$

where $S_M(t) = S_M^0$ for $t < t_0$.

From Equations (3.28 – 30) the volume of money surplus (or shortage) $[M_S(t) - M_D(t)]$ for $t > t_0$ is described by,

$$\frac{d^2}{dt^2}(M_S(t) - M_D(t)) + \mu_P \mu_D \frac{d}{dt}(M_S(t) - M_D(t)) + \mu_P \mu_S (M_S(t) - M_D(t)) = 0 \tag{3.35}$$

with the following initial conditions,

$$M_S(t_0) - M_D(t_0) = -\Delta_M,$$

$$\frac{d}{dt}(M_S(t_0) - M_D(t_0)) = 0.$$

Initial conditions for the money's price $P_M(t)$ are $P_M(t_0) = P_M^0$ and $\frac{dP_M(t_0)}{dt} = \mu_P \, \Delta_M$.

Similar from Equations (3.28 – 30) the money's price $P_M(t)$ is described by the following second-order ordinary differential equation for $t > t_0$,

$$\frac{d^2 P_M(t)}{dt^2} + \mu_P \, \mu_D \frac{dP_M(t)}{dt} + \mu_P \, \mu_S \, P_M(t) + C = 0 \tag{3.36}$$

where $C = -\mu_P \left(\mu_P \, \mu_D \, \Delta_M + \mu_S \, P_M^0 \right)$ is a constant.

If I use new variable $P_2(t) = P_M(t) - P_M^0 - \frac{\mu_P \, \mu_D}{\mu_S} \Delta_M$, Equation (3.36) becomes,

$$\frac{d^2 P_2(t)}{dt^2} + \mu_P \, \mu_D \frac{dP_2(t)}{dt} + \mu_P \, \mu_S \, P_2(t) = 0 \tag{3.37}$$

Hence the initial conditions for $P_2(t)$ are $P_2(t_0) = -\frac{\mu_P \, \mu_D}{\mu_S} \Delta_M$ and $\frac{dP_2(t_0)}{dt} = \mu_P \, \Delta_M$.

Since $M_D(t_0) = M_D^0$ and $\frac{dM_D(t_0)}{dt} = m_D^0$ it takes place from Equation (3.30),

$$M_D(t) = -\mu_D \, P_2(t) + \left(m_D^0 - \mu_P \, \mu_D \, \Delta_M \right)(t - t_0) + M_D^0 - \frac{\mu_P \, \mu_D^2}{\mu_S} \Delta_M \tag{3.38}$$

Equations (3.35) and (3.37) have the same characteristic equation. And the roots of this characteristic equation are,

$$k_{1,2} = -\frac{\mu_P \, \mu_D}{2} \pm \sqrt{\frac{\mu_P^2 \, \mu_D^2}{4} - \mu_P \, \mu_S} \tag{3.39}$$

(a) If $\frac{\mu_P^2 \, \mu_D^2}{4} > \mu_P \, \mu_S$ then both $k_1 < 0$ and $k_2 < 0$.

Hence it takes place for solution of Equation (3.35) $M_S(t) - M_D(t) \to 0$ for $t \to +\infty$. For the similar reason it takes place for solution of Equation (3.37) $P_2(t) \to 0$ for $t \to +\infty$.

From here it takes place for $t \to +\infty$,

$$P_M(t) \to P_M^0 + \frac{\mu_P \mu_D}{\mu_S} \Delta_M \tag{3.40}$$

And it takes place from Equation (3.38) for $t \to +\infty$,

$$M_D(t) \to \left(m_D^0 + \mu_P \mu_D \Delta_M\right)(t - t_0) + M_D^0 - \frac{\mu_P \mu_D^2}{\mu_S} \Delta_M \tag{3.41}$$

Since $M_S(t) - M_D(t) \to 0$ it takes place $M_S(t) \to M_D(t)$ for $t \to +\infty$.

I calculate now the effect of the money's savings by comparing two values taken at the limit $t \to +\infty$ where monetary market comes to equilibrium. The first value is the product $v_M(t) = P_M(t) \times M_D(t)$ of the money's price $P_M(t)$ and the money's demand $M_D(t)$ after savings. The second value is the product $\widetilde{v}_M(t) = \widetilde{P}_M(t) \times \widetilde{M}_D(t)$ of the money's price $\widetilde{P}_M(t) = P_M^0$ and the money's demand $\widetilde{M}_D(t) = m_D^0 (t - t_0) + M_D^0$ if there is no withdrawal of savings from monetary market.

Since $\lim\limits_{t \to +\infty}\left(\frac{P_M(t)}{\widetilde{P}_M(t)}\right) = 1 + \frac{\mu_P \mu_D \Delta_M}{\mu_S P_M^0}$ and $\lim\limits_{t \to +\infty}\left(\frac{M_D(t)}{\widetilde{M}_D(t)}\right) = 1 + \frac{\mu_P \mu_D \Delta_M}{m_D^0}$ it takes place,

$$\lim_{t \to +\infty}\left(\frac{v_M(t)}{\widetilde{v}_M(t)}\right) = \lim_{t \to +\infty}\left(\frac{P_M(t) \times M_D(t)}{\widetilde{P}_M(t) \times \widetilde{M}_D(t)}\right) = 1 + \frac{\mu_P \mu_D \Delta_M}{\mu_S P_M^0 m_D^0}\left(\mu_S P_M^0 + m_D^0 + \mu_P \mu_D \Delta_M\right) \tag{3.42}$$

(b) If $\frac{\mu_P^2 \mu_D^2}{4} = \mu_P \mu_S$ then $k_1 = k_2 = -\frac{\mu_P \mu_D}{2}$.

Hence it takes place for solution of Equation (3.35) $M_S(t) - M_D(t) \to 0$ for $t \to +\infty$.

Similarly it takes place for solution of Equation (3.37) $P_2(t) \to 0$ for $t \to +\infty$.

Then it takes place for $t \to +\infty$,

$$P_M(t) \to P_M^0 + \frac{\mu_P \mu_D}{\mu_S} \Delta_M \tag{3.43}$$

And it takes place from Equation (3.38) for $t \to +\infty$,

$$M_D(t) \to \left(m_D^0 + \mu_P \mu_D \Delta_M\right)(t - t_0) + M_D^0 - \frac{\mu_P \mu_D^2}{\mu_S} \Delta_M \tag{3.44}$$

Since $M_S(t) - M_D(t) \to 0$ it takes place $M_S(t) \to M_D(t)$ for $t \to +\infty$.

Since $\lim_{t \to +\infty}\left(\frac{P_M(t)}{\widetilde{P}_M(t)}\right) = 1 + \frac{\mu_P \mu_D \Delta_M}{\mu_S P_M^0}$ and $\lim_{t \to +\infty}\left(\frac{M_D(t)}{\widetilde{M}_D(t)}\right) = 1 + \frac{\mu_P \mu_D \Delta_M}{m_D^0}$ it takes place,

$$\lim_{t \to +\infty}\left(\frac{v_M(t)}{\widetilde{v}_M(t)}\right) = \lim_{t \to +\infty}\left(\frac{P_M(t) \times M_D(t)}{\widetilde{P}_M(t) \times \widetilde{M}_D(t)}\right) = 1 + \frac{\mu_P \mu_D \Delta_M}{\mu_S P_M^0 m_D^0}\left(\mu_S P_M^0 + m_D^0 + \mu_P \mu_D \Delta_M\right) \tag{3.45}$$

(c) If $\frac{\mu_P^2 \mu_D^2}{4} < \mu_P \mu_S$ then $k_{1,2} = \alpha \pm j\beta$ where $\alpha = -\frac{\mu_P \mu_D}{2}$ and $\beta = \sqrt{\mu_P \mu_S - \frac{\mu_P^2 \mu_D^2}{4}}$.

Thus it takes place for solution of Equation (3.35) $M_S(t) - M_D(t) \to 0$ for $t \to +\infty$. Similarly it takes place for solution of Equation (3.37) $P_2(t) \to 0$ for $t \to +\infty$.

Then it takes place for $t \to +\infty$,

$$P_M(t) \to P_M^0 + \frac{\mu_P \mu_D}{\mu_S}\Delta_M \tag{3.46}$$

And it takes place from Equation (3.38) for $t \to +\infty$,

$$M_D(t) \to \left(m_D^0 + \mu_P \mu_D \Delta_M\right)\left(t - t_0\right) + M_D^0 - \frac{\mu_P \mu_D^2}{\mu_S}\Delta_M \tag{3.47}$$

Since $M_S(t) - M_D(t) \to 0$ it takes place $M_S(t) \to M_D(t)$ for $t \to +\infty$.

Since $\lim_{t \to +\infty}\left(\frac{P_M(t)}{\widetilde{P}_M(t)}\right) = 1 + \frac{\mu_P \mu_D \Delta_M}{\mu_S P_M^0}$ and $\lim_{t \to +\infty}\left(\frac{M_D(t)}{\widetilde{M}_D(t)}\right) = 1 + \frac{\mu_P \mu_D \Delta_M}{m_D^0}$ it takes place,

$$\lim_{t \to +\infty}\left(\frac{v_M(t)}{\widetilde{v}_M(t)}\right) = \lim_{t \to +\infty}\left(\frac{P_M(t) \times M_D(t)}{\widetilde{P}_M(t) \times \widetilde{M}_D(t)}\right) = 1 + \frac{\mu_P \mu_D \Delta_M}{\mu_S P_M^0 m_D^0}\left(\mu_S P_M^0 + m_D^0 + \mu_P \mu_D \Delta_M\right) \tag{3.48}$$

Thus I covered all cases.

Therefore in the limit for $t \to +\infty$ withdrawal of some money from the monetary market cause both an increase in the price of money and an increase of money supply. These actions raise the value $v_M(t)$ of money on the monetary market.

3.2.4 Money Savings and Interest Rates

Thus in previous section I showed that withdrawal of money in the form of savings from the monetary market causes an increase of the money's price. Why does one need to save money from an economic point of view? The answer is following – because she wants to change the monetary savings for the savings of products needed as investments to improve the quality of supplied products and increase their prices.

In previous Chapter I displayed how the products' savings are traded on the secondary market for the monetary savings. Also in Chapter 2 I used the term *interest rate* and loosely identify it with the price of money. Now it is time to describe an interest rate in more details.

Proposition 6 Definition of Interest Rate

Continuous interest rate is defined as proportion of instantaneous changes in the price of money to the price of money at each point in time.

Mathematically it means the following,

$$i_M(t) = \frac{\dot{P}_M(t)}{P_M(t)} \tag{3.49}$$

where $\dot{P}_M(t) = \frac{dP_M(t)}{dt}$.

Now let me look at the changes in interest rate and value of money in following scenarios of savings on the monetary market.

Occasional Savings on Money Market

I described that scenario in the previous section. It increases at time $t = t_0$ the amount of money's savings $S_M(t)$,

$$S_M(t) = \begin{cases} 0, & t < t_0 \\ \Delta_M, & t = t_0 \end{cases} \tag{3.50}$$

where $\Delta_M > 0$.

Here it takes place at the limit for $t \to +\infty$,

$$P_M(t) \to P_M^0 + \frac{\mu_P \mu_D}{\mu_S} \Delta_M \tag{3.51}$$

$$M_D(t) \to \left(m_D^0 + \mu_P \mu_D \Delta_M\right)(t - t_0) + M_D^0 - \frac{\mu_P \mu_D^2}{\mu_S} \Delta_M \tag{3.52}$$

Therefore it takes place for value of money v_M and interest rate $i_M(t)$ for $t \to +\infty$,

$$\lim_{t\to+\infty}\left(\frac{v_M(t)}{\widetilde{v}_M(t)}\right)=1+\frac{\mu_P\,\mu_D\,\Delta_M}{\mu_S\,P_M^0\,m_D^0}\left(\mu_S\,P_M^0+m_D^0+\mu_P\,\mu_D\,\Delta_M\right)>1 \tag{3.53}$$

$$\lim_{t\to+\infty} i_M(t)=\lim_{t\to+\infty}\left(\frac{\dot{P}_M(t)}{P_M(t)}\right)=0 \tag{3.54}$$

Constant-Rate Savings on Money Market

According to this scenario I assume that amount of money's savings $S_M(t)$ increases since time $t=t_0$ according to following formula,

$$S_M(t)=\begin{cases}0, & t<t_0\\ \delta_M\,(t-t_0), & t\ge t_0\end{cases} \tag{3.55}$$

where $\delta_M>0$.

Then Equation (3.28) becomes,

$$\frac{dP_M(t)}{dt}=-\mu_P\left(M_S(t)-M_D(t)-S_M(t)\right) \tag{3.56}$$

Then the savings impact the volume of money surplus (or shortage) on the market in the following way.

Proposition 7 Savings' Impact on Market Surplus (Shortage)

Withdrawal of savings from the market increases the market shortage, and decreases the market surplus.

Mathematically it means the following,

$$D_M(t)=M_S(t)-M_D(t)-S_M(t) \tag{3.57}$$

Hence Equations (3.29, 30, 56) cause that the volume $D_M(t)$ of money surplus (or shortage) for $t>t_0$ is described by,

$$\frac{d^2D_M(t)}{dt^2}+\mu_P\,\mu_D\,\frac{dD_M(t)}{dt}+\mu_P\,\mu_S\,D_M(t)=0 \tag{3.58}$$

with the following initial conditions,

$$D_M(t_0)=0,$$

$$\frac{dD_M(t_0)}{dt}=-\delta_M.$$

Thus it takes place for solution of Equation (3.58) $D_M(t) \to 0$ for $t \to +\infty$.

Initial conditions for the money's price $P_M(t)$ are $P_M(t_0) = P_M^0$ and $\frac{dP_M(t_0)}{dt} = 0$.

Similar the money's price $P_M(t)$ is described by the following second-order ordinary differential equation for $t > t_0$,

$$\frac{d^2 P_M(t)}{dt^2} + \mu_P \mu_D \frac{dP_M(t)}{dt} + \mu_P \mu_S P_M(t) + C = 0 \tag{3.59}$$

where $C = -\mu_P(\mu_S P_M^0 + \delta_M)$ is a constant.

If I use new variable $P_2(t) = P_M(t) - P_M^0 - \frac{1}{\mu_S}\delta_M$, Equation (3.59) becomes,

$$\frac{d^2 P_2(t)}{dt^2} + \mu_P \mu_D \frac{dP_2(t)}{dt} + \mu_P \mu_S P_2(t) = 0 \tag{3.60}$$

Hence the initial conditions for $P_2(t)$ are $P_2(t_0) = -\frac{1}{\mu_S}\delta_M$ and $\frac{dP_2(t_0)}{dt} = 0$.

Since $M_D(t_0) = M_D^0$ and $\frac{dM_D(t_0)}{dt} = m_D^0$ it takes place from Equation (3.30),

$$M_D(t) = -\mu_D P_M(t) + m_D^0 (t - t_0) + M_D^0 + \mu_D P_M^0 \tag{3.61}$$

Therefore it takes place for solution of Equation (3.60) $P_2(t) \to 0$ for $t \to +\infty$. From here it takes place at the limit for $t \to +\infty$,

$$P_M(t) \to P_M^0 + \frac{1}{\mu_S}\delta_M \tag{3.62}$$

$$M_D(t) \to m_D^0 (t - t_0) + M_D^0 - \frac{\mu_D}{\mu_S}\delta_M \tag{3.63}$$

Therefore it takes place for value of money v_M and interest rate $i_M(t)$ for $t \to +\infty$,

$$\lim_{t\to+\infty}\left(\frac{v_M(t)}{\widetilde{v}_M(t)}\right) = \lim_{t\to+\infty}\left(\frac{P_M(t) \times M_D(t)}{\widetilde{P}_M(t) \times \widetilde{M}_D(t)}\right) = 1 + \frac{\delta_M}{\mu_S P_M^0} > 1 \tag{3.64}$$

$$\lim_{t\to+\infty} i_M(t) = \lim_{t\to+\infty}\left(\frac{\dot{P}_M(t)}{P_M(t)}\right) = 0 \tag{3.65}$$

Constant-Acceleration Savings on Money Market

According to this scenario I assume that amount of money's savings $S_M(t)$ increases since time $t = t_0$ according to following formula,

$$S_M(t) = \begin{cases} 0, & t < t_0 \\ \varepsilon_M (t - t_0)^2, & t \geq t_0 \end{cases} \tag{3.66}$$

where $\varepsilon_M > 0$.

Hence Equations (3.29, 30, 56) cause that the volume $D_M(t)$ of money surplus (or shortage) for $t > t_0$ is described by,

$$\frac{d^2 D_M(t)}{dt^2} + \mu_P \mu_D \frac{dD_M(t)}{dt} + \mu_P \mu_S D_M(t) + \varepsilon_M = 0 \tag{3.67}$$

with the following initial conditions,

$$D_M(t_0) = 0,$$

$$\frac{dD_M(t_0)}{dt} = 0.$$

If I use new variable $D_1(t) = D_M(t) + \frac{1}{\mu_P \mu_S}\varepsilon_M$, Equation (3.67) becomes,

$$\frac{d^2 D_1(t)}{dt^2} + \mu_P \mu_D \frac{dD_1(t)}{dt} + \mu_P \mu_S D_1(t) = 0 \tag{3.68}$$

with the following initial conditions,

$$D_1(t_0) = \frac{1}{\mu_P \mu_S}\varepsilon_M,$$

$$\frac{dD_1(t_0)}{dt} = 0.$$

Thus it takes place for solution of Equation (3.68) $D_1(t) \to 0$ for $t \to +\infty$, for solution of Equation (3.67) $D_M(t) \to \dfrac{-1}{\mu_P\,\mu_S}\varepsilon_M$ for $t \to +\infty$.

Initial conditions for the money's price $P_M(t)$ are $P_M(t_0) = P_M^0$ and $\dfrac{dP_M(t_0)}{dt} = 0$.

Similar the money's price $P_M(t)$ is described by the following second-order ordinary differential equation for $t > t_0$,

$$\frac{d^2P_M(t)}{dt^2} + \mu_P\,\mu_D\,\frac{dP_M(t)}{dt} + \mu_P\,\mu_S\,P_M(t) - \mu_P\left[\varepsilon_M\,(t - t_0) + \mu_S\,P_M^0\right] = 0 \qquad (3.69)$$

If I use new variable $P_2(t) = P_M(t) - \dfrac{1}{\mu_S}\varepsilon_M\,(t - t_0) - \left(P_M^0 - \dfrac{\mu_D}{\mu_S^2}\varepsilon_M\right)$, Equation (3.69) becomes,

$$\frac{d^2P_2(t)}{dt^2} + \mu_P\,\mu_D\,\frac{dP_2(t)}{dt} + \mu_P\,\mu_S\,P_2(t) = 0 \qquad (3.70)$$

Hence the initial conditions for $P_2(t)$ are $P_2(t_0) = \dfrac{\mu_D}{\mu_S^2}\varepsilon_M$ and $\dfrac{dP_2(t_0)}{dt} = \dfrac{-1}{\mu_S}\varepsilon_M$.

Since $M_D(t_0) = M_D^0$ and $\dfrac{dM_D(t_0)}{dt} = m_D^0$ it takes place from Equation (3.30),

$$M_D(t) = -\mu_D\,P_M(t) + m_D^0\,(t - t_0) + M_D^0 + \mu_D\,P_M^0 \qquad (3.71)$$

Therefore it takes place for solution of Equation (3.60) $P_2(t) \to 0$ for $t \to +\infty$. From here it takes place at the limit for $t \to +\infty$,

$$P_M(t) \to \frac{1}{\mu_S}\varepsilon_M\,(t - t_0) + \left(P_M^0 - \frac{\mu_D}{\mu_S^2}\varepsilon_M\right) \qquad (3.72)$$

$$M_D(t) \to \left(m_D^0 - \frac{\mu_D}{\mu_S}\varepsilon_M\right)(t - t_0) + M_D^0 + \frac{\mu_D^2}{\mu_S^2}\varepsilon_M \qquad (3.73)$$

Therefore it takes place for value of money v_M and interest rate $i_M(t)$ for $t \to +\infty$,

$$\lim_{t\to+\infty}\left(\frac{v_M(t)}{\tilde{v}_M(t)}\right)=\lim_{t\to+\infty}\left(1-\frac{\mu_D\,\varepsilon_M}{\mu_S\,m_D^0}\right)\left[\frac{\varepsilon_M}{\mu_S\,P_M^0}(t-t_0)+\left(1-\frac{\mu_D\,\varepsilon_M}{\mu_S^2\,P_M^0}\right)\right]=\begin{cases}+\infty, & \varepsilon_M<\frac{\mu_S}{\mu_D}m_D^0\\ 0, & \varepsilon_M=\frac{\mu_S}{\mu_D}m_D^0\\ -\infty & \varepsilon_M>\frac{\mu_S}{\mu_D}m_D^0\end{cases}$$
(3.74)

$$\lim_{t\to+\infty} i_M(t)=\lim_{t\to+\infty}\left(\frac{\dot{P}_M(t)}{P_M(t)}\right)=0$$
(3.75)

Exponential Savings on Money Market

According to this scenario I assume that amount of money's savings $S_M(t)$ increases since time $t=t_0$ according to following formula,

$$S_M(t)=\begin{cases}0, & t<t_0\\ \exp\{\rho_M(t-t_0)\}-1, & t\ge t_0\end{cases}$$
(3.76)

where $\rho_M>0$.

Hence Equations (3.29, 30, 56) cause that the volume $D_M(t)$ of money surplus (or shortage) for $t>t_0$ is described by,

$$\frac{d^2D_M(t)}{dt^2}+\mu_P\,\mu_D\frac{dD_M(t)}{dt}+\mu_P\,\mu_S\,D_M(t)+\rho_M^2\exp\{\rho_M(t-t_0)\}=0$$
(3.77)

with the following initial conditions,

$$D_M(t_0)=0,$$

$$\frac{dD_M(t_0)}{dt}=-\rho_M.$$

If I use new variable $D_1(t)=D_M(t)+\frac{\rho_M^2}{\rho_M^2+\mu_P\,\mu_D\,\rho_M+\mu_P\,\mu_S}\exp\{\rho_M(t-t_0)\}$, Equation (3.77) becomes,

$$\frac{d^2D_1(t)}{dt^2}+\mu_P\,\mu_D\frac{dD_1(t)}{dt}+\mu_P\,\mu_S\,D_1(t)=0$$
(3.78)

with the following initial conditions,

$$D_1(t_0)=\frac{\rho_M^2}{\rho_M^2+\mu_P\,\mu_D\,\rho_M+\mu_P\,\mu_S},$$

$$\frac{dD_1(t_0)}{dt}=-\rho_M+\frac{\rho_M^3}{\rho_M^2+\mu_P\,\mu_D\,\rho_M+\mu_P\,\mu_S}.$$

Thus it takes place for solution of Equation (3.78) $D_1(t)\to 0$ for $t\to+\infty$, for solution of Equation (3.77) $D_M(t)\to\frac{-\rho_M^2}{\rho_M^2+\mu_P\,\mu_D\,\rho_M+\mu_P\,\mu_S}\exp\{\rho_M(t-t_0)\}$ for $t\to+\infty$.

Initial conditions for the money's price $P_M(t)$ are $P_M(t_0)=P_M^0$ and $\frac{dP_M(t_0)}{dt}=0$.

Similar the money's price $P_M(t)$ is described by the following second-order ordinary differential equation for $t>t_0$,

$$\frac{d^2P_M(t)}{dt^2}+\mu_P\,\mu_D\frac{dP_M(t)}{dt}+\mu_P\,\mu_S\,P_M(t)-\mu_P\left[\rho_M\exp\{\rho_M(t-t_0)\}+\mu_S\,P_M^0\right]=0 \tag{3.79}$$

If I use new variable $P_2(t)=P_M(t)-\frac{\mu_P\,\rho_M}{\rho_M^2+\mu_P\,\mu_D\,\rho_M+\mu_P\,\mu_S}\exp\{\rho_M(t-t_0)\}-P_M^0$, Equation (3.79) becomes,

$$\frac{d^2P_2(t)}{dt^2}+\mu_P\,\mu_D\frac{dP_2(t)}{dt}+\mu_P\,\mu_S\,P_2(t)=0 \tag{3.80}$$

Hence the initial conditions for $P_2(t)$ are $P_2(t_0)=\frac{-\mu_P\,\rho_M}{\rho_M^2+\mu_P\,\mu_D\,\rho_M+\mu_P\,\mu_S}$ and $\frac{dP_2(t_0)}{dt}=\frac{-\mu_P\,\rho_M^2}{\rho_M^2+\mu_P\,\mu_D\,\rho_M+\mu_P\,\mu_S}$.

Since $M_D(t_0)=M_D^0$ and $\frac{dM_D(t_0)}{dt}=m_D^0$ it takes place from Equation (3.30),

$$M_D(t)=-\mu_D\,P_M(t)+m_D^0(t-t_0)+M_D^0+\mu_D\,P_M^0 \tag{3.81}$$

Therefore it takes place for solution of Equation (3.80) $P_2(t) \to 0$ for $t \to +\infty$. From here it takes place at the limit for $t \to +\infty$,

$$P_M(t) \to \frac{\mu_P \rho_M}{\rho_M^2 + \mu_P \mu_D \rho_M + \mu_P \mu_S} \exp\{\rho_M (t - t_0)\} + P_M^0 \tag{3.82}$$

$$M_D(t) \to m_D^0 (t - t_0) - \frac{\mu_P \mu_D \rho_M}{\rho_M^2 + \mu_P \mu_D \rho_M + \mu_P \mu_S} \exp\{\rho_M (t - t_0)\} + M_D^0 \tag{3.83}$$

Therefore it takes place for value of money v_M and interest rate $i_M(t)$ for $t \to +\infty$,

$$\lim_{t \to +\infty} \left(\frac{v_M(t)}{\tilde{v}_M(t)} \right) = \lim_{t \to +\infty} \left(\frac{-\mu_P^2 \mu_D \rho_M^2}{\left(\rho_M^2 + \mu_P \mu_D \rho_M + \mu_P \mu_S\right)^2} \times \frac{\exp\{2\rho_M (t - t_0)\}}{P_M^0 m_D^0 (t - t_0)} \right) = -\infty \tag{3.84}$$

$$\lim_{t \to +\infty} i_M(t) = \lim_{t \to +\infty} \left(\frac{\dot{P}_M(t)}{P_M(t)} \right) = \rho_M \tag{3.85}$$

Conclusion about Money Savings and Interest Rates

Thus I can make the following conclusion about interactions between money savings and interest rates.

According to definition, interest rates represent the instantaneous changes of the relative price of money. The price of money changes due to withdrawing some money from the monetary market for the sake of savings. The money savings are done in order to exchange them on the secondary market (market of equities) for the products' savings. The products' savings are created with the purpose of investing them into production process that improves products' qualities and increases their prices.

I described here an economic impact of four different manners of savings – occasional savings at discrete times, savings with a constant rate, savings with a constantly accelerated rate, and savings with a constantly exponential rate.

Occasional savings at discrete time have positive effect on an economic growth. In the long run they increase both the product's price and the amount of product on the market. The economic growth here has a moderate rate.

Savings with a constant rate always create a moderate economic growth as well.

Savings with a constantly accelerated rate make an extreme economic growth or economic recession depending on acceleration rate size. Moderate acceleration rate of savings creates an economic growth whereas strong acceleration rate causes an economic recession.

These three types of savings do not produce a sustained interest rate.

If one imposes a constant interest rate on economy, the latter one to sustain such burden has to make savings with a constantly exponential rate. But performing savings at that rate at a prolonged period of time will eventually drag economy into a severe recession.

3.3 ECONOMIC TRADE

3.3.1 Trade on Integrated Markets of Single Product

When the product is traded on two markets, which are such deeply integrated with each other, so the product on both markets has the same price, one can consider these two markets as one single market.

This situation is essentially similar to intra-industrial dynamics described in Chapter 1.

I will describe here the following scenario.

I assume that the market had been in equilibrium position until time $t = t_0$, the volumes of product's supply $V_{Si}(t)$ and demand $V_{Di}(t)$ on each market were equal, and they all were developing with constant rates r_{Di}^0. The product's price $P_R(t)$ is the same on both markets.

$$V_{Di}(t) = r_{Di}^0 (t - t_0) + V_{Di}^0 \tag{3.86}$$

$$V_{Si}(t) = V_{Di}(t) \tag{3.87}$$

where $V_{Di}(t_0) = V_{Di}^0$ and $i = 1,2$.

At some point in time $t = t_0$ the equilibrium situation was broken, and the product's demand was increased on one of the markets on the amount equal to $\Delta_R > 0$,

$$V_{D1}(t) = \begin{cases} V_{D1}^0 & t = t_0 - 0 \\ V_{D1}^0 + \Delta_R, & t = t_0 \end{cases} \tag{3.88}$$

It would create the economic forces on the markets, which are described by the following system of ordinary differential equations,

$$\frac{dP_R(t)}{dt} = -\lambda_P \left(\sum_{i=1}^{2} V_{Si}(t) - \sum_{i=1}^{2} V_{Di}(t) \right) \tag{3.89}$$

$$\frac{d^2 V_{Si}(t)}{dt^2} = \lambda_{Si} \frac{dP_R(t)}{dt} \tag{3.90}$$

$$\frac{d^2 V_{Di}(t)}{dt^2} = -\lambda_{Di} \frac{d^2 P_R(t)}{dt^2} \tag{3.91}$$

where $t > t_0$.

If one introduces the volumes of total product's supply $V_S(t)=\sum_{i=1}^{2} V_{Si}(t)$ and demand $V_D(t)=\sum_{i=1}^{2} V_{Di}(t)$ on both markets, then from Equations (3.89 – 91) the volume of total product's surplus (or shortage) $[V_S(t)-V_D(t)]$ on both markets for $t > t_0$ is described by,

$$\frac{d^2}{dt^2}(V_S(t)-V_D(t))+\lambda_P\lambda_D\frac{d}{dt}(V_S(t)-V_D(t))+\lambda_P\lambda_S(V_S(t)-V_D(t))=0 \tag{3.92}$$

where $\lambda_S=\sum_{i=1}^{2}\lambda_{Si}$ and $\lambda_D=\sum_{i=1}^{2}\lambda_{Di}$.

Equation (3.92) has the following initial conditions,

$$V_S(t_0)-V_D(t_0)=-\Delta_R,$$

$$\frac{d}{dt}(V_S(t_0)-V_D(t_0))=0.$$

Initial conditions for the product's price $P_R(t)$ are $P_R(t_0)=P_R^0$ and $\frac{dP_R(t_0)}{dt}=\lambda_P\Delta_R$.

Similar from Equations (3.89 – 91) the product's price $P_R(t)$ is described by the following second-order ordinary differential equation for $t > t_0$,

$$\frac{d^2P_R(t)}{dt^2}+\lambda_P\lambda_D\frac{dP_R(t)}{dt}+\lambda_P\lambda_S P_R(t)+C=0 \tag{3.93}$$

where $C=-\lambda_P\left(\lambda_P\lambda_D\Delta_R+\lambda_S P_R^0\right)$ is a constant.

If I use new variable $P_1(t)=P_R(t)-P_R^0-\frac{\lambda_P\lambda_D}{\lambda_S}\Delta_R$, Equation (3.93) becomes,

$$\frac{d^2P_1(t)}{dt^2}+\lambda_P\lambda_D\frac{dP_1(t)}{dt}+\lambda_P\lambda_S P_1(t)=0 \tag{3.94}$$

Therefore the initial conditions for $P_1(t)$ are $P_1(t_0)=-\frac{\lambda_P\lambda_D}{\lambda_S}\Delta_R$ and $\frac{dP_1(t_0)}{dt}=\lambda_P\Delta_R$.

Equations (3.92) and (3.94) have the same characteristic equation. And the roots of this characteristic equation are,

$$k_{1,2} = -\frac{\lambda_P \lambda_D}{2} \pm \sqrt{\frac{\lambda_P^2 \lambda_D^2}{4} - \lambda_P \lambda_S} \tag{3.95}$$

Therefore it takes place $V_S(t) - V_D(t) \to 0$ and $P_1(t) \to 0$ for $t \to +\infty$.

Then for $t \to +\infty$ the volumes of product's supply $V_{Si}(t)$ and demand $V_{Di}(t)$ on each market are described by the following relations,

$$V_{S1}(t) \to \left(r_{D1}^0 + \frac{\lambda_{S1}}{\lambda_S} \lambda_P \lambda_D \Delta_R \right)(t - t_0) + V_{D1}^0 - \frac{\lambda_{S1} \lambda_P \lambda_D^2}{\lambda_S^2} \Delta_R + \frac{\lambda_{S1}}{\lambda_S} \Delta_R \tag{3.96}$$

$$V_{D1}(t) \to \left(r_{D1}^0 + \lambda_P \lambda_{D1} \Delta_R \right)(t - t_0) + V_{D1}^0 - \frac{\lambda_P \lambda_{D1} \lambda_D}{\lambda_S} \Delta_R + \Delta_R \tag{3.97}$$

$$V_{S2}(t) \to \left(r_{D2}^0 + \frac{\lambda_{S2}}{\lambda_S} \lambda_P \lambda_D \Delta_R \right)(t - t_0) + V_{D2}^0 - \frac{\lambda_{S2} \lambda_P \lambda_D^2}{\lambda_S^2} \Delta_R + \frac{\lambda_{S2}}{\lambda_S} \Delta_R \tag{3.98}$$

$$V_{D2}(t) \to \left(r_{D2}^0 + \lambda_P \lambda_{D2} \Delta_R \right)(t - t_0) + V_{D2}^0 - \frac{\lambda_P \lambda_{D2} \lambda_D}{\lambda_S} \Delta_R \tag{3.99}$$

Then there are the following relations between local supply and demand on each market,

$$V_{S1}(t) - V_{D1}(t) \to \frac{\lambda_P \Delta_R}{\lambda_S} (\lambda_{S1} \lambda_{D2} - \lambda_{S2} \lambda_{D1})(t - t_0)$$

$$- \frac{\lambda_P \lambda_D}{\lambda_S^2} \Delta_R (\lambda_{S1} \lambda_{D2} - \lambda_{S2} \lambda_{D1}) - \frac{\lambda_{S2}}{\lambda_S} \Delta_R \tag{3.100}$$

$$V_{S2}(t) - V_{D2}(t) \to \frac{\lambda_P \Delta_R}{\lambda_S} (\lambda_{S2} \lambda_{D1} - \lambda_{S1} \lambda_{D2})(t - t_0)$$

$$- \frac{\lambda_P \lambda_D}{\lambda_S^2} \Delta_R (\lambda_{S2} \lambda_{D1} - \lambda_{S1} \lambda_{D2}) - \frac{\lambda_{S2}}{\lambda_S} \Delta_R \tag{3.101}$$

If $\frac{\lambda_{S1}}{\lambda_{S2}} > \frac{\lambda_{D1}}{\lambda_{D2}}$ then the rate of product's local supply and demand on the first market is positive,

$$\frac{d}{dt}\left(V_{S1}(t) - V_{D1}(t)\right) \to \frac{\lambda_P \Delta_R}{\lambda_S}\left(\lambda_{S1}\lambda_{D2} - \lambda_{S2}\lambda_{D1}\right) > 0 \tag{3.102}$$

It means that local suppliers to the first market are exporting part of the product to the suppliers for the second market.

If $\frac{\lambda_{S1}}{\lambda_{S2}} < \frac{\lambda_{D1}}{\lambda_{D2}}$ then the rate of product's local supply and demand on the first market is negative,

$$\frac{d}{dt}\left(V_{S1}(t) - V_{D1}(t)\right) \to \frac{\lambda_P \Delta_R}{\lambda_S}\left(\lambda_{S1}\lambda_{D2} - \lambda_{S2}\lambda_{D1}\right) < 0 \tag{3.103}$$

It means that suppliers for the first market are importing part of the product from the local suppliers to the second market.

Conditions on the second market are opposite to the ones that exist on the first market.

3.3.2 Trade on Connected Markets of Single Product

When the product is traded on two markets that are separate from each other (for example, because of geographic reason) then the product's price on these markets can be different. That situation creates an opportunity for traders to exploit the price difference and make a profit.

The economic forces created by the price difference for the products on connected markets are trying to eliminate this price difference and bring the markets into equilibrium relative to each other. The main difference between integrated markets and connected markets is that integrated markets instantaneously eliminate any price differences whereas connected markets eliminate price differences gradually.

Then the product's exchange impacts the volume of product's surplus (or shortage) on the product's market in the following way.

Proposition 8 Exchanges' Impact on Product's Market Surplus (Shortage)

Inflow of product on the local market increases the market surplus, and decreases the market shortage. Outflow of product from the local market increases the market shortage, and decreases the market surplus.

Mathematically it means the following,

$$D_{Ri}(t) = V_{Si}(t) + V_{Xi}(t) - V_{Di}(t) \tag{3.104}$$

where $V_{Xi}(t)$ is the volume of product's exchange and $D_{Ri}(t)$ is the volume of product's surplus (or shortage) on the local market.

Now I will describe here the following situation.

I assume that the local markets had been in equilibrium positions until time $t = t_0$, the volumes of product's supply $V_{Si}(t)$ and demand $V_{Di}(t)$ on each market were equal, and they all were developing with constant rates r_{Di}^0. The product's price $P_{Ri}(t) = P_R^0$ was the same on both markets.

$$V_{Di}(t) = r_{Di}^0 (t - t_0) + V_{Di}^0 \tag{3.105}$$

$$V_{Si}(t) = V_{Di}(t) \tag{3.106}$$

where $V_{Di}(t_0) = V_{Di}^0$ and $i = 1,2$.

At some point in time $t = t_0$ the equilibrium situation was broken, and the product's price was increased on one of the markets on the amount equal to $\Delta_P > 0$,

$$P_{R1}(t) = \begin{cases} P_R^0 & t = t_0 - 0 \\ P_R^0 + \Delta_P, & t = t_0 \end{cases} \tag{3.107}$$

Then a trader can withdraw part of the product from the market with lower product's price and put it on the market with higher product's price.

Now let me look at the changes in the product's price and equilibriums on the local markets in following scenarios of product's exchange between connected markets.

One-Time Product's Exchange

According to this scenario I assume the volumes $V_{Xi}(t)$ of product are exchanged between connected markets at time $t = t_0$,

$$V_{X1}(t) = \begin{cases} 0, & t < t_0 \\ \Delta_R, & t = t_0 \end{cases} \tag{3.108}$$

$$V_{X2}(t) = \begin{cases} 0, & t < t_0 \\ -\Delta_R, & t = t_0 \end{cases} \tag{3.109}$$

where $\Delta_R > 0$.

Therefore it takes place at the limit for $t \to +\infty$,

$$P_{R1}(t) \to P_R^0 + \Delta_P - \frac{\lambda_{P1}\lambda_{D1}}{\lambda_{S1}}\Delta_R \tag{3.110}$$

$$P_{R2}(t) \to P_R^0 + \frac{\lambda_{P2}\,\lambda_{D2}}{\lambda_{S2}}\Delta_R \tag{3.111}$$

$$V_{S1}(t) \to \left(r_{D1}^0 - \lambda_{P1}\,\lambda_{D1}\,\Delta_R\right)(t - t_0) + V_{D1}^0 + \frac{\lambda_{P1}\,\lambda_{D1}^2}{\lambda_{S1}}\Delta_R \tag{3.112}$$

$$V_{S2}(t) \to \left(r_{D2}^0 + \lambda_{P2}\,\lambda_{D2}\,\Delta_R\right)(t - t_0) + V_{D2}^0 - \frac{\lambda_{P2}\,\lambda_{D2}^2}{\lambda_{S2}}\Delta_R \tag{3.113}$$

In order to have product's prices equal on both markets $\lim\limits_{t\to+\infty} P_{R1}(t) = \lim\limits_{t\to+\infty} P_{R2}(t)$ it is required,

$$\Delta_R = \left(\frac{\lambda_{P1}\,\lambda_{D1}}{\lambda_{S1}} + \frac{\lambda_{P2}\,\lambda_{D2}}{\lambda_{S2}}\right)^{-1}\Delta_P \tag{3.114}$$

$$\lim_{t\to+\infty} P_{R1}(t) = \lim_{t\to+\infty} P_{R2}(t) = P_R^0 + \frac{\Delta_P}{1 + \dfrac{\lambda_{P1}}{\lambda_{P2}} \times \dfrac{\lambda_{D1}}{\lambda_{D2}} \times \dfrac{\lambda_{S2}}{\lambda_{S1}}} \tag{3.115}$$

$$\lim_{t\to+\infty} V_{S1}(t) = \left(r_{D1}^0 - \frac{\lambda_{S1}\,\Delta_P}{1 + \dfrac{\lambda_{P2}}{\lambda_{P1}} \times \dfrac{\lambda_{D2}}{\lambda_{D1}} \times \dfrac{\lambda_{S1}}{\lambda_{S2}}} \right)(t - t_0) + V_{D1}^0 + \frac{\lambda_{D1}\,\Delta_P}{1 + \dfrac{\lambda_{P2}}{\lambda_{P1}} \times \dfrac{\lambda_{D2}}{\lambda_{D1}} \times \dfrac{\lambda_{S1}}{\lambda_{S2}}} \tag{3.116}$$

$$\lim_{t\to+\infty} V_{S2}(t) = \left(r_{D2}^0 + \frac{\lambda_{S2}\,\Delta_P}{1 + \dfrac{\lambda_{P1}}{\lambda_{P2}} \times \dfrac{\lambda_{D1}}{\lambda_{D2}} \times \dfrac{\lambda_{S2}}{\lambda_{S1}}} \right)(t - t_0) + V_{D2}^0 - \frac{\lambda_{D2}\,\Delta_P}{1 + \dfrac{\lambda_{P1}}{\lambda_{P2}} \times \dfrac{\lambda_{D1}}{\lambda_{D2}} \times \dfrac{\lambda_{S2}}{\lambda_{S1}}} \tag{3.117}$$

Constant-Rate Product's Exchange

According to this scenario I assume the volumes $V_{Xi}(t)$ of product are exchanged between connected markets starting at time $t = t_0$,

$$V_{X1}(t) = \begin{cases} 0, & t < t_0 \\ \delta_R\,(t - t_0), & t \ge t_0 \end{cases} \tag{3.118}$$

$$V_{X2}(t)=\begin{cases} 0, & t<t_0 \\ -\delta_R(t-t_0), & t\geq t_0 \end{cases} \tag{3.119}$$

where $\delta_R > 0$.

Therefore it takes place at the limit for $t \to +\infty$,

$$P_{R1}(t)\to P_R^0+\Delta_P-\frac{1}{\lambda_{S1}}\delta_R \tag{3.120}$$

$$P_{R2}(t)\to P_R^0+\frac{1}{\lambda_{S2}}\delta_R \tag{3.121}$$

$$V_{S1}(t)\to\left(r_{D1}^0-\delta_R\right)(t-t_0)+V_{D1}^0+\frac{\lambda_{D1}}{\lambda_{S1}}\delta_R \tag{3.122}$$

$$V_{S2}(t)\to\left(r_{D2}^0+\delta_P\right)(t-t_0)+V_{D2}^0-\frac{\lambda_{D2}}{\lambda_{S2}}\delta_P \tag{3.123}$$

In order to have product's prices equal on both markets $\lim_{t\to+\infty}P_{R1}(t)=\lim_{t\to+\infty}P_{R2}(t)$ it is required,

$$\delta_R=\left(\frac{1}{\lambda_{S1}}+\frac{1}{\lambda_{S2}}\right)^{-1}\Delta_P \tag{3.124}$$

$$\lim_{t\to+\infty}P_{R1}(t)=\lim_{t\to+\infty}P_{R2}(t)=P_R^0+\frac{\Delta_P}{1+\dfrac{\lambda_{S2}}{\lambda_{S1}}} \tag{3.125}$$

$$\lim_{t\to+\infty}V_{S1}(t)=\left(r_{D1}^0-\frac{\Delta_P}{\dfrac{1}{\lambda_{S1}}+\dfrac{1}{\lambda_{S2}}}\right)(t-t_0)+V_{D1}^0+\frac{\lambda_{D1}\Delta_P}{1+\dfrac{\lambda_{S1}}{\lambda_{S2}}} \tag{3.126}$$

$$\lim_{t\to+\infty} V_{S2}(t) = \left(r_{D2}^0 + \frac{\Delta_P}{\frac{1}{\lambda_{S1}} + \frac{1}{\lambda_{S2}}} \right)(t - t_0) + V_{D2}^0 - \frac{\lambda_{D2}\Delta_P}{1 + \frac{\lambda_{S2}}{\lambda_{S1}}} \tag{3.127}$$

3.3.3 Trade on Foreign Exchange Market

To understand the process of establishing the exchange rates between different currencies one has to comprehend deeper what are the prices of products in general and the price of money as a peculiar product in particular.

As I said earlier I use here as the price of product a dimensionless quantity, which can be regarded as a relative price. The words above are related to the price of money as well, which is just another kind of product even of a peculiar nature. However when I am talking here about price relativity I imply the relativity in time i.e. the current product's price relative to the product's price at some particular point in time. When I want to talk about current exchange rates between different currencies I mean the relative prices of different moneys (currencies) where relativity is taken rather in space (i.e. one currency relative to another currency) then in time.

Thus the following statement defines *exchange rate* between different currencies.

Proposition 9 Definition of Exchange Rate

Continuous exchange rate between two currencies (moneys) is defined as proportion of the price of one currency (money) to the price of another currency (money) at each point in time.

Mathematically it means the following,

$$x_{ij}(t) = \frac{P_{Mi}(t)}{P_{Mj}(t)} \tag{3.128}$$

where $P_{Mi}(t)$ and $P_{Mj}(t)$ are the prices of moneys on different monetary markets, $j \neq i$.

Now let me look at the changes in exchange rate and value of moneys caused by the money's trade between two monetary markets.

When the money volumes are traded between two monetary markets it creates the economic forces, which are changing the price of moneys on these monetary markets. And the changes in the prices of moneys drive the changes in the monetary exchange rates.

Then the exchange of monetary volumes impacts the volume of money surplus (or shortage) on each monetary market in the following way.

Proposition 10 Exchanges' Impact on Money's Market Surplus (Shortage)

Inflow of money on the local monetary market increases the money market surplus, and decreases the money market shortage. Outflow of money from the local monetary market increases the money market shortage, and decreases the money market surplus.

Mathematically it means the following,

$$D_{Mi}(t) = M_{Si}(t) + M_{Xi}(t) - M_{Di}(t) \tag{3.129}$$

where $M_{Xi}(t)$ is the volume of monetary exchange and $D_{Mi}(t)$ is the volume of money's surplus (or shortage) on the local monetary market

Now I will describe here the following situation.

I assume that the local monetary markets had been in equilibrium positions until time $t = t_0$, the volumes of money's supply $M_{Si}(t)$ and demand $M_{Di}(t)$ on each market were equal, and they all were developing with constant rates m^0_{Di}. The prices of moneys $P_{Mi}(t) = P^0_{Mi}$ were constants on both markets.

$$M_{Di}(t) = m^0_{Di}(t - t_0) + M^0_{Di} \tag{3.130}$$

$$M_{Si}(t) = M_{Di}(t) \tag{3.131}$$

where $M_{Di}(t_0) = M^0_{Di}$ and $i = 1, 2$.

Therefore initial condition at time $t = t_0$ for exchange rates was $x_{ij}(t_0) = \dfrac{P^0_{Mi}}{P^0_{Mj}}$.

One-Time Money's Exchange

At some point in time $t = t_0$ the equilibrium situation was broken, and the monetary amount equal to $\Delta_M > 0$ (let me say, for neutrality expressed in third-party denominations) was brought to the first local market and corresponding monetary amount equal to $-\Delta_M < 0$ (expressed in the same third-party denominations) was withdrawn from the second local market,

$$M_{X1}(t) = \begin{cases} 0, & t < t_0 \\ \Delta_M, & t = t_0 \end{cases} \tag{3.132}$$

$$M_{X2}(t) = \begin{cases} 0, & t < t_0 \\ -\Delta_M, & t = t_0 \end{cases} \tag{3.133}$$

where $\Delta_M > 0$.

Therefore since $P_{Mi}(t) = P^0_{Mi}$, $\dfrac{dP_{M1}(t)}{dt} = -\mu_{P1}\Delta_M$, $\dfrac{dP_{M2}(t)}{dt} = \mu_{P2}\Delta_M$, $\dfrac{dD_{Mi}(t)}{dt} = 0$ it takes place at the limit for $t \to +\infty$,

$$\lim_{t\to+\infty} P_{M1}(t) = P_{M1}(t_0) - \frac{1}{\mu_{S1}}\left[\frac{dD_{M1}(t_0)}{dt} - \mu_{D1}\frac{dP_{M1}(t_0)}{dt}\right] = P_{M1}^0 - \frac{\mu_{P1}\,\mu_{D1}}{\mu_{S1}}\Delta_M \tag{3.134}$$

$$\lim_{t\to+\infty} P_{M2}(t) = P_{M2}(t_0) - \frac{1}{\mu_{S2}}\left[\frac{dD_{M2}(t_0)}{dt} - \mu_{D2}\frac{dP_{M2}(t_0)}{dt}\right] = P_{M2}^0 + \frac{\mu_{P2}\,\mu_{D2}}{\mu_{S2}}\Delta_M \tag{3.135}$$

$$\lim_{t\to+\infty} x_{12}(t) = \lim_{t\to+\infty}\frac{P_{M1}(t)}{P_{M2}(t)} = x_{12}(t_0)\times\frac{1-\dfrac{\mu_{P1}\,\mu_{D1}}{\mu_{S1}}\times\dfrac{\Delta_M}{P_{M1}^0}}{1+\dfrac{\mu_{P2}\,\mu_{D2}}{\mu_{S2}}\times\dfrac{\Delta_M}{P_{M2}^0}} < x_{12}(t_0) \tag{3.136}$$

Thus at the limit for $t \to +\infty$ the relative price $x_{12}(t)$ of first currency relative to the second currency decreases as a result of one-time increase of the money's surplus on the first local monetary market. At the same limit for $t \to +\infty$ the relative price $x_{21}(t)$ of second currency relative to the first currency increases as a result of one-time increase of the money's shortage on the second local monetary market.

Constant-Rate Money's Exchange

At some point in time $t = t_0$ the equilibrium situation was broken, and since that time the monetary amount with a constant rate equal to $\delta_M > 0$ (let me say, for neutrality expressed in third-party denominations) was brought to the first local market and the monetary amount with a constant rate equal to $-\delta_M < 0$ (expressed in the same third-party denominations) was withdrawn from the second local market,

$$M_{X1}(t) = \begin{cases} 0, & t < t_0 \\ \delta_M(t-t_0), & t \ge t_0 \end{cases} \tag{3.137}$$

$$M_{X2}(t) = \begin{cases} 0, & t < t_0 \\ -\delta_M(t-t_0), & t = t_0 \end{cases} \tag{3.138}$$

where $\delta_M > 0$.

Therefore since $P_{Mi}(t) = P_{Mi}^0$, $\dfrac{dP_{Mi}(t)}{dt} = 0$, $\dfrac{dD_{M1}(t)}{dt} = \delta_M$, $\dfrac{dD_{M2}(t)}{dt} = -\delta_M$ it takes place at the limit for $t \to +\infty$,

$$\lim_{t\to+\infty} P_{M1}(t) = P_{M1}(t_0) - \frac{1}{\mu_{S1}}\left[\frac{dD_{M1}(t_0)}{dt} - \mu_{D1}\frac{dP_{M1}(t_0)}{dt}\right] = P_{M1}^0 - \frac{1}{\mu_{S1}}\delta_M \tag{3.139}$$

$$\lim_{t\to+\infty} P_{M2}(t) = P_{M2}(t_0) - \frac{1}{\mu_{S2}}\left[\frac{dD_{M2}(t_0)}{dt} - \mu_{D2}\frac{dP_{M2}(t_0)}{dt}\right] = P_{M2}^0 + \frac{1}{\mu_{S2}}\delta_M \tag{3.140}$$

$$\lim_{t\to+\infty} x_{12}(t) = \lim_{t\to+\infty}\frac{P_{M1}(t)}{P_{M2}(t)} = x_{12}(t_0)\times\frac{1-\frac{1}{\mu_{S1}}\times\frac{\delta_M}{P_{M1}^0}}{1+\frac{1}{\mu_{S2}}\times\frac{\delta_M}{P_{M2}^0}} < x_{12}(t_0) \tag{3.141}$$

Thus at the limit for $t \to +\infty$ the relative price $x_{12}(t)$ of first currency relative to the second currency decreases as a result of constant-rate increase of the money's surplus on the first local monetary market. At the same limit for $t \to +\infty$ the relative price $x_{21}(t)$ of second currency relative to the first currency increases as a result of constant-rate increase of the money's shortage on the second local monetary market.

3.4 Market Arbitrage

3.4.1 Outline of Arbitration Phenomenon

Economic markets are not functioning in the closed forms; they are connected with outside economic world. And conditions on the local markets are influenced by the prevailing conditions in the outside economic world. When economic conditions on the local market do not coincide with prevailing conditions in the outside world, there emerge economic forces on the local market, which are trying to bring the economic conditions on the local market with an agreement with prevailing global economic conditions.

The abovementioned process is called *a market arbitrage*. I will describe here two kinds of market arbitrage.

The first one is an alignment of the products' prices, existing on the local market, with the prices on the same products, prevailing on the global market.

The second one is an alignment of the money's price, existing on the local monetary market, with the money's price, prevailing on the global monetary market.

3.4.2 Product's Price Arbitrage

As I said before when the economic conditions on the local market do not coincide with prevailing conditions on the global market, there appear economic forces trying to align the local conditions with prevailing global conditions. That process is called a market arbitrage.

One example of market arbitrage is an alignment of local prices with prevailing global prices on the same products. That alignment is performed through the products' exchange between local and global markets where products' exchanges are driven by the special economic forces, which I call here *the products' exchange forces*.

I make the following assumption about dynamics of products' exchange forces.

Hypothesis 9 Behavior of Product's Exchange Force

When the price of product on the local market is not equal to the global price of product, it creates the disturbing "product's exchange force", which affects the rate of product's exchange between local and global markets. The rate of product's exchange at each point in time is linearly proportional to the surplus (or shortage) of product's price on the local market relative to the product's price on the global market.

Mathematically the statement above can be described by the following expression,

$$\frac{dV_X(t)}{dt} = \lambda_X \left(P_R(t) - P_{RG}(t)\right) \tag{3.142}$$

where $\lambda_X > 0$, $P_R(t)$ and $P_{RG}(t)$ are the product's prices on the local and global markets.

I will describe the work of product's exchange forces by following example of the product's price growth.

I assume that the local market itself had been in equilibrium position and also it had been in equilibrium position with regard to the global market until time $t = t_0$, i.e. the volumes of product's supply $V_S(t)$ and demand $V_D(t)$ on local market were equal, and they were developing with constant rates r_D^0. The product's price $P_R(t) = P_{RG}^0$ on the local market was constant and the same as on the global market. There were no product's exchanges between local and global markets, i.e. $V_X(t) = 0$.

$$V_D(t) = r_D^0 (t - t_0) + V_D^0 \tag{3.143}$$

$$V_S(t) = V_D(t) \tag{3.144}$$

where $V_D(t_0) = V_D^0$.

At some point in time $t = t_0$ the equilibrium situation was broken, and the product's price on the local market had increased on the amount equal to $\Delta_{PR} > 0$,

$$P_R(t) = \begin{cases} P_{RG}^0, & t = t_0 - 0 \\ P_{RG}^0 + \Delta_{PR}, & t = t_0 \end{cases} \tag{3.145}$$

It will create the economic forces, which are described by the following ordinary differential equations,

$$\frac{dP_R(t)}{dt} = -\lambda_P \left(V_S(t) + V_X(t) - V_D(t)\right) \tag{3.146}$$

$$\frac{d^2V_S(t)}{dt^2} = \lambda_S \frac{dP_R(t)}{dt} \tag{3.147}$$

$$\frac{d^2V_D(t)}{dt^2} = -\lambda_D \frac{d^2P_R(t)}{dt^2} \tag{3.148}$$

$$\frac{dV_X(t)}{dt} = \lambda_X \left(P_R(t) - P_{RG}(t)\right) \tag{3.149}$$

In Equations (3.146 – 149) above the values $\lambda_P, \lambda_S, \lambda_D, \lambda_X \geq 0$ are constants.

Then the product's shortage (surplus) $D_R(t) = V_S(t) + V_X(t) - V_D(t)$ on the local market is described by the following second-order ordinary differential equation for $t > t_0$,

$$\frac{d^2D_R(t)}{dt^2} + \lambda_P \lambda_D \frac{dD_R(t)}{dt} + \lambda_P \left(\lambda_S + \lambda_X\right) D_R(t) = 0 \tag{3.150}$$

and initial values for the product's shortage (surplus) $D_R(t)$ are $D_R(t_0) = 0$, $\frac{dD_R(t_0)}{dt} = \lambda_X \Delta_{PR}$.

Similarly the product's price $P_R(t)$ is described by the following second-order ordinary differential equation for $t > t_0$,

$$\frac{d^2P_R(t)}{dt^2} + \lambda_P \lambda_D \frac{dP_R(t)}{dt} + \lambda_P \left(\lambda_S + \lambda_X\right)\left(P_R(t) - P_{RG}^0 - \frac{\lambda_S}{\lambda_S + \lambda_X} \Delta_{PR}\right) = 0 \tag{3.151}$$

where initial conditions for the product's price $P_R(t)$ are $P_R(t_0) = P_{RG}^0 + \Delta_{PR}$, $\frac{dP_R(t_0)}{dt} = 0$.

If I use new variable $P_1(t) = P_R(t) - P_{RG}^0 - \frac{\lambda_S}{\lambda_S + \lambda_X} \Delta_{PR}$, Equation (3.151) becomes,

$$\frac{d^2P_1(t)}{dt^2} + \lambda_P \lambda_D \frac{dP_1(t)}{dt} + \lambda_P \left(\lambda_S + \lambda_X\right) P_1(t) = 0 \tag{3.152}$$

Therefore the initial conditions for $P_1(t)$ are $P_1(t_0) = \frac{\lambda_X}{\lambda_S + \lambda_X} \Delta_{PR}$ and $\frac{dP_1(t_0)}{dt} = 0$.

The roots of characteristic equation corresponding to Equations (3.150) and (3.152) are,

$$k_{1,2} = -\frac{\lambda_P \lambda_D}{2} \pm \sqrt{\frac{\lambda_P^2 \lambda_D^2}{4} - \lambda_P \left(\lambda_S + \lambda_X\right)} \tag{3.153}$$

Therefore at the limit for $t \to +\infty$ it takes place $D_R(t) \to 0$ and $P_1(t) \to 0$ and it is fulfilled,

$$P_R(t) \to P_{RG}^0 + \frac{\lambda_S}{\lambda_S + \lambda_X} \Delta_{PR} \tag{3.154}$$

$$V_X(t) \to \frac{\lambda_S \Delta_{PR}}{1 + \frac{\lambda_S}{\lambda_X}} (t - t_0) \tag{3.155}$$

$$V_D(t) \to r_D^0 (t - t_0) + V_D^0 + \frac{\lambda_X}{\lambda_S + \lambda_X} \lambda_D \Delta_{PR} \tag{3.156}$$

$$V_S(t) \to \left(r_D^0 - \frac{\lambda_S \Delta_{PR}}{1 + \frac{\lambda_S}{\lambda_X}} \right) (t - t_0) + V_D^0 + \frac{\lambda_X}{\lambda_S + \lambda_X} \lambda_D \Delta_{PR} \tag{3.157}$$

The results above may be economically interpreted as verification that a wealthy country can never eliminate a trade deficit. Besides if the capacity of local market is much smaller than the capacity of global market (in situation here, $0 < \lambda_S << \lambda_X$) then it takes place $\frac{\lambda_S}{\lambda_S + \lambda_X} \approx 0$, and it is $\lim_{t \to +\infty} P_R(t) \approx P_{RG}^0$, $\lim_{t \to +\infty} \frac{dV_X(t)}{dt} \approx \lambda_S \Delta_{PR}$, $\lim_{t \to +\infty} \frac{dV_D(t)}{dt} = r_D^0$, $\lim_{t \to +\infty} \frac{dV_S(t)}{dt} \approx r_D^0 - \lambda_S \Delta_{PR}$.

3.4.3 Money's Price Arbitrage

Another example of market arbitrage is an alignment of money's price rate that exists on the local monetary market with the money's price prevailing on the global monetary market. That alignment is performed through the money's exchange between local and global monetary markets where money's exchanges are driven by the special economic forces, which I call here *the money's exchange forces*.

I make the following assumption about dynamics of money's exchange forces.

Hypothesis 10 Behavior of Money's Exchange Force

When the price of money on the local monetary market is not equal to the global price of money, it creates the disturbing "money's exchange force", which affects the rate of money's exchange between local and global monetary markets. The rate of money's exchange at each point in time is linearly proportional to the surplus (or shortage) of money's price on the local monetary market relative to the money's price on the global monetary market.

Mathematically the statement above can be described by the following expression,

$$\frac{dM_X(t)}{dt} = \mu_X\left(P_M(t) - P_{MG}(t)\right) \tag{3.158}$$

where $\mu_X > 0$, $P_M(t)$ and $P_{MG}(t)$ are the money's prices on the local and global monetary markets.

I will describe the work of money's exchange forces by following example of the money's price growth.

I assume that the local monetary market itself had been in equilibrium position and also it had been in equilibrium position with regard to the global monetary market until time $t = t_0$, i.e. the volumes of money's supply $M_S(t)$ and demand $M_D(t)$ on local monetary market were equal, and they were developing with constant rates m_D^0. The money's price $P_M(t) = P_{MG}^0$ on the local monetary market was constant and the same as on the global monetary market. There were no money's exchanges between local and global monetary markets, i.e. $M_X(t) = 0$.

$$M_D(t) = m_D^0(t - t_0) + M_D^0 \tag{3.159}$$

$$M_S(t) = M_D(t) \tag{3.160}$$

where $M_D(t_0) = M_D^0$.

At some point in time $t = t_0$ the equilibrium situation was broken, and the money's price on the local monetary market had increased on the amount equal to $\Delta_{PM} > 0$,

$$P_M(t) = \begin{cases} P_{MG}^0, & t = t_0 - 0 \\ P_{MG}^0 + \Delta_{PM}, & t = t_0 \end{cases} \tag{3.161}$$

It will create the economic forces, which are described by the following ordinary differential equations,

$$\frac{dP_M(t)}{dt} = -\mu_P\left(M_S(t) + M_X(t) - M_D(t)\right) \tag{3.162}$$

$$\frac{d^2M_S(t)}{dt^2} = \mu_S \frac{dP_M(t)}{dt} \tag{3.163}$$

$$\frac{d^2M_D(t)}{dt^2} = -\mu_D \frac{d^2P_M(t)}{dt^2} \tag{3.164}$$

$$\frac{dM_X(t)}{dt} = \mu_X \left(P_M(t) - P_{MG}(t)\right) \tag{3.165}$$

In Equations (3.162 – 165) above the values $\mu_P, \mu_S, \mu_D, \mu_X \geq 0$ are constants.

The money's shortage (surplus) $D_M(t) = M_S(t) + M_X(t) - M_D(t)$ on the local monetary market is described by the following second-order ordinary differential equation for $t > t_0$,

$$\frac{d^2D_M(t)}{dt^2} + \mu_P \mu_D \frac{dD_M(t)}{dt} + \mu_P (\mu_S + \mu_X) D_M(t) = 0 \tag{3.166}$$

and initial values for money's shortage (surplus) $D_M(t)$ are $D_M(t_0) = 0$, $\frac{dD_M(t_0)}{dt} = \mu_X \Delta_{PM}$.

Similarly the money's price $P_M(t)$ is described by the following second-order ordinary differential equation for $t > t_0$,

$$\frac{d^2P_M(t)}{dt^2} + \mu_P \mu_D \frac{dP_M(t)}{dt} + \mu_P (\mu_S + \mu_X)\left(P_M(t) - P_{MG}^0 - \frac{\mu_S}{\mu_S + \mu_X} \Delta_{PM} \right) = 0 \tag{3.167}$$

where initial conditions for the money's price $P_M(t)$ are $P_M(t_0) = P_{MG}^0 + \Delta_{PM}$, $\frac{dP_M(t_0)}{dt} = 0$.

If I use new variable $P_2(t) = P_M(t) - P_{MG}^0 - \frac{\mu_S}{\mu_S + \mu_X} \Delta_{PM}$, Equation (3.167) becomes,

$$\frac{d^2P_2(t)}{dt^2} + \mu_P \mu_D \frac{dP_2(t)}{dt} + \mu_P (\mu_S + \mu_X) P_2(t) = 0 \tag{3.168}$$

Therefore the initial conditions for $P_2(t)$ are $P_2(t_0) = \frac{\mu_X}{\mu_S + \mu_X} \Delta_{PM}$ and $\frac{dP_2(t_0)}{dt} = 0$.

The roots of characteristic equation corresponding to Equations (3.166) and (3.168) are,

$$k_{1,2} = -\frac{\mu_P \mu_D}{2} \pm \sqrt{\frac{\mu_P^2 \mu_D^2}{4} - \mu_P(\mu_S + \mu_X)} \tag{3.169}$$

Therefore at the limit for $t \to +\infty$ it takes place $D_M(t) \to 0$ and $P_2(t) \to 0$ and it is fulfilled,

$$P_M(t) \to P_{MG}^0 + \frac{\mu_S}{\mu_S + \mu_X} \Delta_{PM} \tag{3.170}$$

$$M_X(t) \to \frac{\mu_S \Delta_{PM}}{1 + \frac{\mu_S}{\mu_X}}(t - t_0) \tag{3.171}$$

$$M_D(t) \to m_D^0 (t - t_0) + M_D^0 + \frac{\mu_X}{\mu_S + \mu_X} \mu_D \Delta_{PM} \tag{3.172}$$

$$M_S(t) \to \left(m_D^0 - \frac{\mu_S \Delta_{PM}}{1 + \frac{\mu_S}{\mu_X}} \right)(t - t_0) + M_D^0 + \frac{\mu_X}{\mu_S + \mu_X} \mu_D \Delta_{PM} \tag{3.173}$$

The results above may be economically interpreted as verification that country with a strong currency always has a capital inflow from the global monetary market. Besides if the capacity of local monetary market is much smaller than the capacity of global monetary market (in situation here, $0 < \mu_S << \mu_X$) then it takes place $\frac{\mu_S}{\mu_S + \mu_X} \approx 0$, and it is $\lim_{t \to +\infty} P_M(t) \approx P_{MG}^0$, $\lim_{t \to +\infty} \frac{dM_X(t)}{dt} \approx \mu_S \Delta_{PM}$, $\lim_{t \to +\infty} \frac{dM_D(t)}{dt} = m_D^0$, $\lim_{t \to +\infty} \frac{dM_S(t)}{dt} \approx m_D^0 - \mu_S \Delta_{PM}$.

3.4.4 About Interest Rate Arbitrage

Some economists talk about interest rate arbitrage as well by using the following logical construction.

They say if an interest rate on the local monetary market exceeds the interest rate on the global monetary market, there appear economic forces, which try to eliminate the difference in the interest rates above. These economic forces drive inflow of the capital from global monetary market into local monetary market that creates a surplus of the capital on the local monetary market that drives down interest rate on the local monetary market, and eventually eliminates the mentioned difference between local and global interest rates. However the aforesaid logical construction is wrong from the mathematical point of view.

As I showed before, to keep a continuous-time interest rate constant it is required to sustain an exponential savings on the local monetary market. It causes the money's shortage on the local monetary market, where the money's shortage above is described by an exponential function. On the other hand, the effect of arbitrage between local and global monetary markets can be majorized by a constant-acceleration function. Since the exponential function always dominates any finite-power series at infinity, the aforementioned difference in interest rates between local and global monetary markets can never be eliminated through a market arbitrage mechanism.

3.5 Summary

In the last Chapter I described the concepts of economic growth, economic trade, and market arbitrage.

I described that economic growth is caused by products' and money's savings. I also presented mathematical models that connect different kinds of economic growth with particular rates of products' and money's savings.

I presented mathematical models describing an economic trade between distinct markets that have the same or different prices for same products. I also portrayed the trade on foreign exchange market and described dynamics of the exchange rate between different currencies.

I defined the market arbitrage as an alignment of economic conditions existing on the local market with corresponding economic conditions prevailing on the global market. I presented mathematical models showing the market arbitrage mechanism both on the market of products, and on the monetary market.

That concludes the book. In appendices I portray the time-space business fluctuations, and apply the concept of market arbitrage to the task of securities valuations.

Appendix A

TIME-SPACE FLUCTUATIONS

A.1 INTRODUCTION

Here I briefly describe real business cycles that fluctuate both in time and in space. This material originally was presented in [11].

A.2 EQUILIBRIUM STATE

Let me consider an economical model with one product that is traded on the market. The market is characterized by its situation at each point t in time and at each point x in one-dimensional space.

I denote $V_S(x,t)$ – the volume of the product's supply in point x at time t, $V_D(x,t)$ – the volume of the product's demand in point x at time t, and $P_R(x,t)$ – the product's price in point x at time t.

I assume that market was at equilibrium position in each point in space until time $t = t_0$, i.e. in every point x the volumes of product's supply $V_S(x,t)$ and demand $V_D(x,t)$ on the market were equal, and they both were developing with constant rate r_D^0,

$$V_D(x,t) = r_D^0 (t - t_0) + V_D^0 \tag{A.1}$$

$$V_S(x,t) = V_D(x,t) \tag{A.2}$$

where $V_D(x,t_0) = V_D^0$ and $\forall x$.

A.3 Dynamics in Time Domain

I assume that at some point in time $t = t_0$ the equilibrium situation was broken in point $x = x_0$, and the product's demand at this point $x = x_0$ was increased on the amount of product equal to $\Delta_R > 0$,

$$V_D(x_0,t) = \begin{cases} V_D^0, & t = t_0 - 0 \\ V_D^0 + \Delta_R, & t = t_0 \end{cases} \tag{A.3}$$

I denote $D_R(x,t) = V_S(x,t) - V_D(x,t)$ – the product's shortage (surplus) on the market in point x at time t. Then the scenario above would create on the market in point $x = x_0$ at time $t = t_0$ the product's shortage $D_R(x_0,t_0) = -\Delta_R$ causing economic forces, which act to bring the market at this point $x = x_0$ to a new equilibrium position.

If I denote c – the velocity of the product's shortage (surplus) distributing on the market, then the market at point $x = x_1 \geq x_0$ would start experiencing the product's shortage (surplus) at time $t_1 = t_0 + \frac{x_1 - x_0}{c} \geq t_0$.

Aforesaid economic forces are described by the following ordinary differential equations regarding to the product's supply $V_S(x,t)$, demand $V_D(x,t)$, and price $P_R(x,t)$ in point $x = x_1$,

$$\frac{dP_R(x_1,t)}{dt} = -\lambda_P \left(V_S(x_1,t) - V_D(x_1,t)\right) \tag{A.4}$$

$$\frac{d^2 V_S(x_1,t)}{dt^2} = \lambda_S \frac{dP_R(x_1,t)}{dt} \tag{A.5}$$

$$\frac{d^2 V_D(x_1,t)}{dt^2} = -\lambda_D \frac{d^2 P_R(x_1,t)}{dt^2} \tag{A.6}$$

where the values $\lambda_P, \lambda_S, \lambda_D \geq 0$ are constants, $x_1 \geq x_0$ and $t > t_1$.

I can rewrite Equations (A.4 – 6) above to describe dynamics of product's shortage (surplus) $D_R(x_1,t)$ on the market at each point $x_1 \geq x_0$ for $t > t_1$,

$$\frac{d^2 D_R(x_1,t)}{dt^2} + \lambda_P \lambda_D \frac{dD_R(x_1,t)}{dt} + \lambda_P \lambda_S D_R(x_1,t) = 0 \tag{A.7}$$

where $D_R(x_1,t_1)$ and $\frac{dD_R(x_1,t_1)}{dt}$ are initials values that I will explain in the next section.

Since the roots of characteristic equation that corresponds to Equation (A.7) are,

$$k_{1,2} = -\frac{\lambda_P \lambda_D}{2} \pm \sqrt{\frac{\lambda_P^2 \lambda_D^2}{4} - \lambda_P \lambda_S} \tag{A.8}$$

it takes place $D_R(x_1,t) = V_S(x_1,t) - V_D(x_1,t) \to 0$ for $t \to +\infty$ and $\forall x_1$.

A.4 Dynamics in Space Domain

When the equilibrium situation on the market was broken in point $x = x_0$ at time $t = t_0$, there appear also economic forces, which cause the product's shortage (surplus) to spread to other points $x = x_1$ of the market as well.

Since c – the velocity of the product's shortage (surplus) distributing on the market, then the market at point $x = x_1 \geq x_0$ would start experiencing the product's shortage (surplus) at time $t_1 = t_0 + \frac{x_1 - x_0}{c} \geq t_0$.

The economic forces above are described by the following ordinary differential equations regarding to the product's supply $V_S(x,t)$, demand $V_D(x,t)$, and price $P_R(x,t)$ at time $t = t_1$,

$$\frac{dP_R(x,t_1)}{dx} = -\nu_P \left(V_S(x,t_1) - V_D(x,t_1)\right) \tag{A.9}$$

$$\frac{d^2 V_S(x,t_1)}{dx^2} = \nu_S \frac{dP_R(x,t_1)}{dx} \tag{A.10}$$

$$\frac{d^2 V_D(x,t_1)}{dx^2} = -\nu_D \frac{d^2 P_R(x,t_1)}{dx^2} \tag{A.11}$$

where the values $\nu_P, \nu_S, \nu_D \geq 0$ are constants, $t_1 \geq t_0$ and $x_0 \leq x \leq x_1$.

I can rewrite Equations (A.9 – 11) above to describe dynamics of product's shortage (surplus) $D_R(x,t_1)$ on the market at each moment $t_1 \geq t_0$ for $x_0 \leq x \leq x_1$,

$$\frac{d^2 D_R(x,t_1)}{dx^2} + \nu_P \nu_D \frac{dD_R(x,t_1)}{dx} + \nu_P \nu_S D_R(x,t_1) = 0 \tag{A.12}$$

If I take according to above chosen scenario $D_R(x_0,t_0) = -\Delta_R$ and $\frac{dD_R(x_0,t_0)}{dx} = 0$ as initials values for Equation (A.12), I can find the initials values $D_R(x_1,t_1)$ from Equation (A.12) and take $\frac{dD_R(x_1,t_1)}{dt} = 0$ for time fluctuations, and use them in Equation (A.7) for each $x_1 \geq x_0$ and $t_1 = t_0 + \frac{x_1 - x_0}{c} \geq t_0$.

Since the roots of characteristic equation that corresponds to Equation (A.12) are,

$$k_{1,2} = -\frac{\nu_P \nu_D}{2} \pm \sqrt{\frac{\nu_P^2 \nu_D^2}{4} - \nu_P \nu_S} \tag{A.13}$$

it takes place $D_R(x,t_1) = V_S(x,t_1) - V_D(x,t_1) \to 0$ for $x \to +\infty$ and $t_1 = t_0 + \frac{x - x_0}{c}$.

A.5 Dynamics of Prices

Similar from Equations (A.9 – 11) according to above chosen scenario the product's price $P_R(x,t_1)$ is described by the following second-order ordinary differential equation at each moment $t_1 \geq t_0$ for $x_0 \leq x \leq x_1$,

$$\frac{d^2 P_R(x,t_1)}{dx^2} + \nu_P \nu_D \frac{dP_R(x,t_1)}{dx} + \nu_P \nu_S \left(P_R(x,t_1) - P_R(x_0,t_0) - \frac{\nu_P \nu_D}{\nu_S} \Delta_R \right) = 0 \tag{A.14}$$

Hence it takes place $P_R(x,t_1) \to P_R(x_0,t_0) + \frac{\nu_P \nu_D}{\nu_S} \Delta_R$ when $x \to +\infty$ for each $t_1 \geq t_0$.

If I take in line with above chosen scenario $P_R(x_0,t_0) = P_R^0$ and $\frac{dP_R(x_0,t_0)}{dx} = \nu_P \Delta_R$ as initials values for Equation (A.14), I can find the initials values $P_R(x_1,t_1)$ from Equation

(A.14) and $\frac{dP_R(x_1,t_1)}{dt} = -\lambda_P D_R(x_1,t_1)$ from Equation (A.12) for time fluctuations for $x_1 \geq x_0$ and $t_1 = t_0 + \frac{x_1 - x_0}{c} \geq t_0$.

Comparable from Equations (A.4 – 6) the product's price $P_R(x,t)$ is described by the following second-order ordinary differential equation at $x_1 \geq x_0$ for all $t > t_1 = t_0 + \frac{x_1 - x_0}{c}$,

$$\frac{d^2 P_R(x_1,t)}{dt^2} + \lambda_P \lambda_D \frac{dP_R(x_1,t)}{dt} + \lambda_P \lambda_S \left(P_R(x_1,t) - P_R(x_1,t_1) + \frac{\lambda_P \lambda_D}{\lambda_S} D_R(x_1,t_1) \right) = 0 \qquad \text{(A.15)}$$

Hence it takes place $P_R(x_1,t) \to P_R(x_1,t_1) - \frac{\lambda_P \lambda_D}{\lambda_S} D_R(x_1,t_1)$ when $t \to +\infty$ for $x_1 \geq x_0$.

A.6 Economic Forces in Space Domain

In Chapter 3 I described the economic forces causing the products' exchange between markets where markets were considering without dimension in space.

If one wants to describe situation on the markets with continuous characteristics in the space domain, she has to employ approach outlined briefly in this appendix.

Appendix B

SECURITIES VALUATION

B.1 INTRODUCTION

In this appendix I outline the approach solving the practical task of evaluating several kinds of securities such as common-stock shares and stock options. In particular I describe such stock options as American call and put options and European call and put options.

I chose to present the examples of shares and stock options valuations since they are a good illustration of the arbitrage mechanism. Part of the material was introduced in [14] and [21].

B.2 SUSTAINED STATE

B.2.1 Constant-Rate Growth of Money Value

Let me consider an economical model of the monetary market with the growing value of money. As I explained in Chapter 3 the constant-value continuous interest rate is not sustainable from the theoretical point of view.

I assume that the value of money has a constant-value growth rate,

$$P_M(t) = \varepsilon_M (t - t_0) + P_M^0 \tag{B.1}$$

where $\varepsilon_M > 0$ and $P_M(t_0) = P_M^0$.

Such situation as was shown in Chapter 3 corresponds to constant-acceleration savings on the monetary market, where acceleration rate is relatively small and linearly proportional to the value ε_M.

B.2.2 About Exponential Growth of Money Value

Some economists argue that constant-rate growth of money value can be transformed to exponential growth of money value,

$$P_M(t_0 + nT) = P_M^0 (1 + r)^n \tag{B.2}$$

where $r = \frac{\varepsilon T}{P_M^0}$ is relative rate of money growth over one time interval T and $n = 0,1,2,\ldots$, if one reinvests and compounds the money's amount at discrete time intervals $T, 2T, 3T, \ldots$.

However to preserve the exponential growth of money value, the economy has to maintain the exponential growth of savings, which is not sustainable.

Indeed, if the price of money $P_M(t)$ is described by Equation (B.2) then,

$$P_M(t) = P_M^0 (1 + r)^\tau \tag{B.3}$$

where $\tau = \frac{t - t_0}{T}$.

Nevertheless though the price of money cannot constantly grow exponentially, nothing prevents some relatively small amounts of money from growing exponentially over relatively short periods of time.

B.3 Common-Stock Share's Value

I described the approach to assess equities in Chapter 2. To apply it to the valuation of common-stock shares one needs to account for an arbitrage between the market of money and the market of equities (actually there are also arbitrages caused by the company's liquidation value and by the company's takeover value but I don't consider them in this book).

Let me denote $P_{SEC}(t)$ – the market price of shares, $P_{PR}(t)$ – the market price of the company's product, and $P_M(t)$ – the market price of money. I also introduce $V_{SEC\_S}(t)$ – supply of shares on the market, $V_{SEC\_D}(t)$ –demand for shares on the market, and $M_{SEC}(t)$ – inflow of money on the market of common-stock shares due to arbitrage. Then ordinary differential equations describing the economic forces on the market of common-stock shares are,

$$\frac{dP_{SEC}(t)}{dt} = -\lambda_{SEC\_P} \left(V_{SEC\_S}(t) - V_{SEC\_D}(t) - M_{SEC}(t) \right) \tag{B.4}$$

$$\frac{d^2V_{SEC\_S}(t)}{dt^2} = \lambda_{SEC\_S}\frac{dP_{SEC}(t)}{dt} \tag{B.5}$$

$$\frac{d^2V_{SEC\_D}(t)}{dt^2} = -\lambda_{SEC\_D}\frac{d^2P_{SEC}(t)}{dt^2} + \lambda_{SEC\_PR}\frac{dP_{PR}(t)}{dt} \tag{B.6}$$

$$\frac{d^2M_{SEC}(t)}{dt^2} = \mu_{SEC}\left(\frac{dP_{SEC}(t)}{dt} - \frac{dP_M(t)}{dt}\right) \tag{B.7}$$

In Equations (B.4 – 7) above the values $\lambda_{SEC\_P}, \lambda_{SEC\_S}, \lambda_{SEC\_D}, \lambda_{SEC\_PR}, \mu_{SEC} \geq 0$ are constants.

Here is the meaning of Equations (B.7). When the price of shares grows faster then the price of money, it creates an economic force that drives inflow of money on the market of these particular equities. When the price of shares grows slower then the price of money, it drives the outflow of money from the market of these particular equities.

B.4 AMERICAN CALL OPTION'S VALUE

I described the approach to assess derivatives in Chapter 2. To apply it to an American call option valuation one needs to account for an arbitrage between the market of money and the market of derivatives, and for an arbitrage relating the price of American call option and its intrinsic value. On the other hand, the price of stock options doesn't have direct relationship with the price of company's product.

Let me denote $P_{AC}(t)$ – the market price of American call option. I also denote $\hat{P}_{AC}(t)$ – the intrinsic value of American call option,

$$\hat{P}_{AC}(t) = P_{SEC}(t) - P_{AC\_STR} \tag{B.8}$$

where P_{AC_STR} is the strike price of American call option, $P_{SEC}(t)$ – the market price of underlying security, and $\hat{P}_{AC}(t) \geq 0$.

I also introduce $V_{AC\_S}(t)$ – supply of American call options on the market, $V_{AC\_D}(t)$ – demand for American call options on the market, $V_{AC\_X}(t)$ – inflow of American call options on the market due to arbitrage, and $M_{AC}(t)$ – inflow of money on the market of American call options due to arbitrage. Then ordinary differential equations describing the economic forces on the market of American call options are,

$$\frac{dP_{AC}(t)}{dt} = -\lambda_{AC\_P}\left(V_{AC\_S}(t) + V_{AC\_X}(t) - V_{AC\_D}(t) - M_{AC}(t)\right) \tag{B.9}$$

$$\frac{d^2V_{AC\_S}(t)}{dt^2} = \lambda_{AC\_S}\frac{dP_{AC}(t)}{dt} \tag{B.10}$$

$$\frac{d^2V_{AC\_D}(t)}{dt^2} = -\lambda_{AC\_D}\frac{d^2P_{AC}(t)}{dt^2} \tag{B.11}$$

$$\frac{dV_{AC\_X}(t)}{dt} = \lambda_{AC\_X}\left(P_{AC}(t) - \hat{P}_{AC}(t)\right) \tag{B.12}$$

$$\frac{d^2M_{AC}(t)}{dt^2} = \mu_{AC}\left(\frac{dP_{AC}(t)}{dt} - \frac{dP_M(t)}{dt}\right) \tag{B.13}$$

$$0 \le P_{AC}(t) \le P_{SEC}(t) \tag{B.14}$$

In Equations (B.9 – 13) above the values $\lambda_{AC\_P}, \lambda_{AC\_S}, \lambda_{AC\_D}, \lambda_{AC\_X}, \mu_{AC} \ge 0$ are constants.[2]

The meaning of Equation (B.12) is following. When the price of American call option exceeds its intrinsic value, it creates economic force, which drives the inflow of new American call options on the market of derivatives. When the price of American call option goes below its intrinsic value, it drives the outflow of American call options from the market of derivatives.

Here is the meaning of Equation (B.13). When the price of American call option grows faster then the price of money, it creates an economic force that drives inflow of money on the market of these particular derivatives. When the price of American call option grows slower then the price of money, it drives the outflow of money from the market of these particular derivatives.

[2] Theoretically speaking Equation (B.11) should look like following,

$$\frac{d^2V_{AC\_D}(t)}{dt^2} = -\lambda_{AC\_D}\frac{d^2P_{AC}(t)}{dt^2} + \lambda_{AC\_SEC}\frac{dP_{SEC}(t)}{dt} + \lambda_{AC\_PR}\frac{dP_{PR}(t)}{dt}$$

i.e. demand for American call options is positively affected by changes in the price of underlying security $P_{SEC}(t)$ and in the price of product $P_{PR}(t)$ (as usual, values $\lambda_{AC\_SEC}, \lambda_{AC\_PR} \ge 0$ are constants). However such impact is (in most situations) insignificant since a usual pattern here is as follows – the product's price $P_{PR}(t)$ affects the price of security $P_{SEC}(t)$, which in turn affects the intrinsic value of American call option $\hat{P}_{AC}(t)$, and through an arbitrage mechanism that determines the price of American call $P_{AC}(t)$.

The meaning of Inequality (B.14) is that price of American call option cannot exceed the price of underlying security.

B.5 AMERICAN PUT OPTION'S VALUE

Let me denote $P_{AP}(t)$ – the market price of American put option. I also denote $\hat{P}_{AP}(t)$ – the intrinsic value of American put option,

$$\hat{P}_{AP}(t) = P_{AP\_STR} - P_{SEC}(t) \quad \text{(B.15)}$$

where P_{AP_STR} is the strike price of American put option, $P_{SEC}(t)$ – the market price of underlying security, and $\hat{P}_{AP}(t) \geq 0$.

I also introduce $V_{AP\_S}(t)$ – supply of American put options on the market, $V_{AP\_D}(t)$ – demand for American put options on the market, $V_{AP\_X}(t)$ – inflow of American put options on the market due to arbitrage, and $M_{AP}(t)$ – inflow of money on the market of American put options due to arbitrage. Then ordinary differential equations describing the economic forces on the market of American put options are,

$$\frac{dP_{AP}(t)}{dt} = -\lambda_{AP\_P}\left(V_{AP\_S}(t) + V_{AP\_X}(t) - V_{AP\_D}(t) - M_{AP}(t)\right) \quad \text{(B.16)}$$

$$\frac{d^2 V_{AP\_S}(t)}{dt^2} = \lambda_{AP\_S}\frac{dP_{AP}(t)}{dt} \quad \text{(B.17)}$$

$$\frac{d^2 V_{AP\_D}(t)}{dt^2} = -\lambda_{AP\_D}\frac{d^2 P_{AP}(t)}{dt^2} \quad \text{(B.18)}$$

$$\frac{dV_{AP\_X}(t)}{dt} = \lambda_{AP\_X}\left(P_{AP}(t) - \hat{P}_{AP}(t)\right) \quad \text{(B.19)}$$

$$\frac{d^2 M_{AP}(t)}{dt^2} = \mu_{AP}\left(\frac{dP_{AP}(t)}{dt} - \frac{dP_M(t)}{dt}\right) \quad \text{(B.20)}$$

$$0 \leq P_{AP}(t) \leq P_{AP\_STR} \quad \text{(B.21)}$$

In Equations (B.16 – 20) above the values $\lambda_{AP\_P}, \lambda_{AP\_S}, \lambda_{AP\_D}, \lambda_{AP\_X}, \mu_{AP} \geq 0$ are constants.[3]

The meaning of Equation (B.19) is following. When the price of American put option exceeds its intrinsic value, it creates economic force, which drives the inflow of new American put options on the market of derivatives. When the price of American put option goes below its intrinsic value, it drives the outflow of American put options from the market of derivatives.

Here is the meaning of Equation (B.20). When the price of American put option grows faster then the price of money, it creates an economic force that drives inflow of money on the market of these particular derivatives. When the price of American put option grows slower then the price of money, it drives the outflow of money from the market of these particular derivatives.

The meaning of Inequality (B.21) is that price of American put option cannot exceed the option's strike price.

B.6 European Call Option's Value

Let me denote $P_{EC}(t)$ – the market price of European call option, where the option matures at time $t = t_1$. I also denote $\hat{P}_{EC}(t)$ – the intrinsic value of European call option.

The intrinsic value of European call option determined at maturity is,

$$\hat{P}_{EC}(t_1) = P_{SEC}(t_1) - P_{EC\_STR} \tag{B.22}$$

where P_{EC_STR} is the strike price of European call option, $P_{SEC}(t_1)$ – the market price of underlying security at time $t = t_1$, and $\hat{P}_{EC}(t_1) \geq 0$.

The intrinsic value of European call option at time $t \leq t_1$ is,

[3] Theoretically speaking Equation (B.18) should look like following,

$$\frac{d^2 V_{AP\_D}(t)}{dt^2} = -\lambda_{AP\_D} \frac{d^2 P_{AP}(t)}{dt^2} - \lambda_{AP\_SEC} \frac{dP_{SEC}(t)}{dt} - \lambda_{AP\_PR} \frac{dP_{PR}(t)}{dt}$$

i.e. demand for American put options is negatively affected by changes in the price of underlying security $P_{SEC}(t)$ and in the price of product $P_{PR}(t)$ (as usual, values $\lambda_{AP\_SEC}, \lambda_{AP\_PR} \geq 0$ are constants). However such impact is (in most situations) insignificant since a usual pattern here is as follows – the product's price $P_{PR}(t)$ affects the price of security $P_{SEC}(t)$, which in turn affects the intrinsic value of American put option $\hat{P}_{AP}(t)$, and through an arbitrage mechanism that determines the price of American put $P_{AP}(t)$.

$$\hat{P}_{EC}(t) = P_{SEC}(t) - \frac{1}{1 + d(t_1(t))} P_{EC\_STR} \tag{B.23}$$

where $\hat{P}_{EC}(t) \geq 0$, and $d(t_1(t)) - \frac{P_M(t_1(t)) - P_M(t)}{P_M(t)}$ is discount coefficient equal to the market-expected at time t relative growth of money value until time $t = t_1$, $P_M(t_1(t))$ is the market-expected at time t the value of money at time $t = t_1$.

There are few words about the value $P_M(t_1(t))$. It is determined by $\frac{dP_M(t)}{dt}$ – the current change of money's value, by the current and expected economic forces on local monetary market caused respectively by the money's supply, demand, and savings, and by the arbitrage between local and global monetary markets.

Since I express the practical task of evaluating stock options in this appendix, I can put commonly used exponential growth of money value in Equation (B.23) (though economy cannot sustain such growth for a long period of time it is possible to have it for relatively small amounts of money over relatively short periods of time),

$$\hat{P}_{EC}(t) = P_{SEC}(t) - \frac{1}{(1 + r)^{\tau}} P_{EC\_STR} \tag{B.24}$$

where r is relative rate of money growth over one time interval T, $\tau = \frac{t_1 - t}{T}$ is number of time intervals until option's maturity, and $P_{SEC}(t)$ – the market price of underlying security at time t.

I also introduce $V_{EC\_S}(t)$ – supply of European call options on the market, $V_{EC\_D}(t)$ – demand for European call options on the market, $V_{EC\_X}(t)$ – inflow of European call options on the market due to arbitrage, and $M_{EC}(t)$ – inflow of money on the market of European call options due to arbitrage. Then ordinary differential equations describing the economic forces on the market of European call options are,

$$\frac{dP_{EC}(t)}{dt} = -\lambda_{EC\_P}\left(V_{EC\_S}(t) + V_{EC\_X}(t) - V_{EC\_D}(t) - M_{EC}(t)\right) \tag{B.25}$$

$$\frac{d^2 V_{EC\_S}(t)}{dt^2} = \lambda_{EC\_S} \frac{dP_{EC}(t)}{dt} \tag{B.26}$$

$$\frac{d^2 V_{EC\_D}(t)}{dt^2} = -\lambda_{EC\_D} \frac{d^2 P_{EC}(t)}{dt^2} \tag{B.27}$$

$$\frac{dV_{EC\_X}(t)}{dt} = \lambda_{EC\_X}\left(P_{EC}(t) - \hat{P}_{EC}(t)\right) \tag{B.28}$$

$$\frac{d^2 M_{EC}(t)}{dt^2} = \mu_{EC}\left(\frac{dP_{EC}(t)}{dt} - \frac{dP_M(t)}{dt}\right) \tag{B.29}$$

$$0 \le P_{EC}(t) \le P_{SEC}(t) \tag{B.30}$$

In Equations (B.25 – 29) above the values $\lambda_{EC\_P}, \lambda_{EC\_S}, \lambda_{EC\_D}, \lambda_{EC\_X}, \mu_{EC} \ge 0$ are constants.[4]

The meaning of Equation (B.28) is following. When the price of European call option exceeds its intrinsic value, it creates economic force, which drives the inflow of new European call options on the market of derivatives. When the price of European call option goes below its intrinsic value, it drives the outflow of European call options from the market of derivatives.

Here is the meaning of Equation (B.29). When the price of European call option grows faster then the price of money, it creates an economic force that drives inflow of money on the market of these particular derivatives. When the price of European call option grows slower then the price of money, it drives the outflow of money from the market of these particular derivatives.

The meaning of Inequality (B.30) is that price of European call option cannot exceed the price of underlying security.

B.7 European Put Option's Value

Let me denote $P_{EP}(t)$ – the market price of European put option, where the option matures at time $t = t_1$. I also denote $\hat{P}_{EP}(t)$ – the intrinsic value of European put option.

The intrinsic value of European put option determined at maturity is,

---

[4] Theoretically speaking Equation (B.27) should look like following,

$$\frac{d^2 V_{EC\_D}(t)}{dt^2} = -\lambda_{EC\_D}\frac{d^2 P_{EC}(t)}{dt^2} + \lambda_{EC\_SEC}\frac{dP_{SEC}(t)}{dt} + \lambda_{EC\_PR}\frac{dP_{PR}(t)}{dt}$$

i.e. demand for European call options is positively affected by changes in the price of underlying security $P_{SEC}(t)$ and in the price of product $P_{PR}(t)$ (as usual, values $\lambda_{EC\_SEC}, \lambda_{EC\_PR} \ge 0$ are constants). However such impact is (in most situations) insignificant since a usual pattern here is as follows – the product's price $P_{PR}(t)$ affects the price of security $P_{SEC}(t)$, which in turn affects the intrinsic value of European call option $\hat{P}_{EC}(t)$, and through an arbitrage mechanism that determines the price of European call $P_{EC}(t)$.

$$\hat{P}_{EP}(t_1) = P_{EP\_STR} - P_{SEC}(t_1) \tag{B.31}$$

where P_{EP_STR} is the strike price of European put option, $P_{SEC}(t_1)$ – the market price of underlying security at time $t = t_1$, and $\hat{P}_{EP}(t_1) \geq 0$.

The intrinsic value of European put option at time $t \leq t_1$ is,

$$\hat{P}_{EP}(t) = \frac{1}{1 + d(t_1(t))} P_{EP\_STR} - P_{SEC}(t) \tag{B.32}$$

where $\hat{P}_{EP}(t) \geq 0$, and $d(t_1(t)) = \frac{P_M(t_1(t)) - P_M(t)}{P_M(t)}$ is discount coefficient equal to the market-expected at time t relative growth of money value until time $t = t_1$, $P_M(t_1(t))$ is the market-expected at time t the value of money at time $t = t_1$.

Since I express the practical task of evaluating stock options in this appendix, I can put commonly used exponential growth of money value in Equation (B.32),

$$\hat{P}_{EP}(t) = \frac{1}{(1 + r)^{\tau}} P_{EP\_STR} - P_{SEC}(t) \tag{B.33}$$

where r is relative rate of money growth over one time interval T, $\tau = \frac{t_1 - t}{T}$ is number of time intervals until option's maturity, and $P_{SEC}(t)$ – the market price of underlying security at time t.

I also introduce $V_{EP\_S}(t)$ – supply of European put options on the market, $V_{EP\_P}(t)$ – demand for European put options on the market, $V_{EP\_X}(t)$ – inflow of European put options on the market due to arbitrage, and $M_{EP}(t)$ – inflow of money on the market of European put options due to arbitrage. Then ordinary differential equations describing the economic forces on the market of European put options are,

$$\frac{dP_{EP}(t)}{dt} = -\lambda_{EP\_P}\left(V_{EP\_S}(t) + V_{EP\_X}(t) - V_{EP\_D}(t) - M_{EP}(t)\right) \tag{B.34}$$

$$\frac{d^2 V_{EP\_S}(t)}{dt^2} = \lambda_{EP\_S} \frac{dP_{EP}(t)}{dt} \tag{B.35}$$

$$\frac{d^2V_{EP\_D}(t)}{dt^2} = -\lambda_{EP\_D}\frac{d^2P_{EP}(t)}{dt^2} \tag{B.36}$$

$$\frac{dV_{EP\_X}(t)}{dt} = \lambda_{EP\_X}\left(P_{EP}(t) - \hat{P}_{EP}(t)\right) \tag{B.37}$$

$$\frac{d^2M_{EP}(t)}{dt^2} = \mu_{EP}\left(\frac{dP_{EP}(t)}{dt} - \frac{dP_M(t)}{dt}\right) \tag{B.38}$$

$$0 \le P_{EP}(t) \le \frac{1}{1+d(t_1(t))}P_{STR} \tag{B.39}$$

In Equations (B.34 – 38) above the values $\lambda_{EP\_P}, \lambda_{EP\_S}, \lambda_{EP\_D}, \lambda_{EP\_X}, \mu_{EP} \ge 0$ are constants.[5]

The meaning of Equation (B.37) is following. When the price of European put option exceeds its intrinsic value, it creates economic force, which drives the inflow of new European put options on the market of derivatives. When the price of European put option goes below its intrinsic value, it drives the outflow of European put options from the market of derivatives.

Here is the meaning of Equation (B.38). When the price of European put option grows faster then the price of money, it creates an economic force that drives inflow of money on the market of these particular derivatives. When the price of European put option grows slower then the price of money, it drives the outflow of money from the market of these particular derivatives.

The meaning of Inequality (B.39) is that price of European put option cannot exceed the option's discounted strike price.

[5] Theoretically speaking Equation (B.36) should look like following,

$$\frac{d^2V_{EP\_D}(t)}{dt^2} = -\lambda_{EP\_D}\frac{d^2P_{EP}(t)}{dt^2} - \lambda_{EP\_SEC}\frac{dP_{SEC}(t)}{dt} - \lambda_{EP\_PR}\frac{dP_{PR}(t)}{dt}$$

i.e. demand for European put options is negatively affected by changes in the price of underlying security $P_{SEC}(t)$ and in the price of product $P_{PR}(t)$ (as usual, values $\lambda_{EP\_SEC}, \lambda_{EP\_PR} \ge 0$ are constants). However such impact is (in most situations) insignificant since a usual pattern here is as follows – the product's price $P_{PR}(t)$ affects the price of security $P_{SEC}(t)$, which in turn affects the intrinsic value of European put option $\hat{P}_{EP}(t)$, and through an arbitrage mechanism that determines the price of European put $P_{EP}(t)$.

B.8 ARBITRAGE BETWEEN CURRENT AND FUTURE VALUES

Sometimes there are following situations on the stock market. There come news at time t about company's prosperous outlook for some time $t = t_1$ in the future, and stock suddenly jumps. What kind of mechanism works in this particular development?

The answer is that in situation above there are acting economic forces created by the arbitrage that relates the market price of particular security $P_{SEC}(t)$ at time t and the discounted expected price of that security $\hat{P}_{SEC}(t) = \frac{1}{1 + d(t_1(t))} P_{SEC}(t_1)$ at time $t = t_1$, where $d(t_1(t))$ is a discount coefficient equal to the market-expected relative growth of money from time t until time $t = t_1$,

$$\frac{dV_{SEC\_X}(t)}{dt} = \lambda_{SEC\_X}\left(P_{SEC}(t) - \hat{P}_{SEC}(t)\right) \tag{B.40}$$

where $V_{SEC\_X}(t)$ – arbitration demand for securities on the market, and $\lambda_{SEC\_X} \geq 0$.[6]

Here is the meaning of Equation (B.40). When the discounted future price $\hat{P}_{SEC}(t)$ exceeds the current price of security $P_{SEC}(t)$, the value $V_{SEC\_X}(t)$ is decreasing. Therefore the securities' shortage on the market $D_{SEC}(t) = V_{SEC\_S}(t) + V_{SEC\_X}(t) - V_{SEC\_D}(t)$ is increasing (or surplus is decreasing) that drives the price of security $P_{SEC}(t)$ up. When the discounted future price $\hat{P}_{SEC}(t)$ goes below the current price of security $P_{SEC}(t)$, the value $V_{SEC\_X}(t)$ is increasing. Hence the securities' surplus $D_{SEC}(t)$ on the market is increasing (or shortage is decreasing) that drives the price of security $P_{SEC}(t)$ down.

---

[6] In most situations the current economic dynamics, which includes current price $P_{SEC}(t)$, affects future prices $\hat{P}_{SEC}(t)$ through acting market forces and inertia of economic system. However in occasional situation projected future economic circumstances could affect the current state of economy. For example, prediction regarding to looming drop in future oil production could affect the current price of oil on markets.

REFERENCES

[1] V. I. Arnol'd, *"Ordinary Differential Equations,"* 3rd ed., Springer Verlag, Berlin; New York, 1992.

[2] F. R. Gantmacher, *"The Theory of Matrices,"* vol. 1 and 2, Chelsea Publishing Co, New York, 1959.

[3] A. Krouglov, *"Determination of the Lower and Upper Bounds for Savings Circulating in National Economy and Impact of These Bounds on the Economy's Growth or Drop," ewp-mac/9706008*, available at http://econwpa.wustl.edu.

[4] A. Krouglov, *"Mathematical Model of Simple Business Fluctuations," ewp-mac/9706009*, available at http://econwpa.wustl.edu.

[5] A. Krouglov, *"Mathematical Model of Interdependency between Production and Price Fluctuations," ewp-mac/9709002*, available at http://econwpa.wustl.edu.

[6] A. Krouglov, *"Mathematical Description of Business Fluctuations," ewp-mac/9710002*, available at http://econwpa.wustl.edu.

[7] A. Krouglov, *"Continuous-Time Model of Business Fluctuations, and Optimal Behavior of an Interest Rate," ewp-mac/9802023*, available at http://econwpa.wustl.edu.

[8] A. Krouglov, *"Dynamics of Business Fluctuations in the Leontief-Type Economy," ewp-mac/9807007*, available at http://econwpa.wustl.edu.

[9] A. Krouglov, *"Mathematical Model of the Inflationary Process," ewp-mac/9804001*, available at http://econwpa.wustl.edu.

[10] A. Krouglov, *"Mathematical Model of Competitive Impacts between Business Entities," ewp-mic/9903003*, availablc at http://cconwpa.wustl.cdu.

[11] A. Krouglov, *"Time-Space Model of Business Fluctuations," ewp-mac/0004008*, available at http://econwpa.wustl.edu.

[12] A. Krouglov, *"Mathematical Model of the Inflationary Process (Part II)," ewp-mac/0301010*, available at http://econwpa.wustl.edu.

[13] A. Krouglov, *"Dynamical Elements of the Monetary Theory," ewp-mac/0306013*, available at http://econwpa.wustl.edu.

[14] A. Krouglov, *"Mathematical Model of Stock Market Fluctuations in the Absence of Economic Growth," ewp-mac/0402022*, available at http://econwpa.wustl.edu.

[15] A. Krouglov, *"Dynamical Elements of the Monetary Theory," in "Trends in Macroeconomics Research,"* L. Z. Pelzer, Ed., Nova Science Publishers, New York, 2005.

[16] W. Leontief, *"The Structure of the American Economy 1919-1939: An Empirical Application of Equilibrium Analysis,"* Oxford University Press, New York, 1951.

[17] W. Leontief et al., *"Studies in the Structure of the American Economy,"* Oxford University Press, New York, 1953.

[18] I. G. Petrovski, *"Ordinary Differential Equations,"* Prentice Hall, Englewoods Cliffs, NJ, 1966.

[19] N. S. Piskunov, "*Differential and Integral Calculus*," Groningen P. Noordhoff, 1965.

[20] L. S. Pontryagin, *"Ordinary Differential Equations,"* Addison-Wesley, Reading, MA, 1962.

[21] A. Krouglov, *"Mathematical Model of Stock Market Fluctuations in the Absence of Economic Growth,"* in *"New Developments in Macroeconomics Research,"* L. Z. Pelzer, Ed., Nova Science Publishers, New York, 2006 (forthcoming).

INDEX

T

V

W